55 ways

TO THE WILDERNESS
IN SOUTHCENTRAL ALASKA

By Helen Nienhueser and Nancy Simmerman

THE MOUNTAINEERS and
MOUNTAINEERING CLUB OF ALASKA

Second edition

THE MOUNTAINEERS

Organized 1906

To explore and study the mountains, forests, and
watercourses of the Northwest;

To gather into permanent form the history and
traditions of this region;

To preserve by the encouragement of protective legislation
or otherwise the natural beauty of Northwest America;

To make expeditions into these regions in fulfillment
of the above purposes;

To encourage a spirit of good fellowship among all
lovers of outdoor life.

MOUNTAINEERING CLUB OF ALASKA

Organized 1958

To promote the enjoyment of hiking, climbing, and
exploration of the mountains;

Cultivation of mountain-climbing skills and techniques;

To teach and encourage mountain safety;

Maintenance of a trained group to be available for
technical assistance to mountain rescue;

To assist in the prevention of waste and unnecessary
destruction of the natural scene.

First edition, June 1972; Revised, June 1975
Second edition, December 1978; Revised July 1981
Copyright© 1972, 1978, 1981 by The Mountaineers

Published by The Mountaineers
715 Pike Street
Seattle, Washington 98101
Book design by Marge Mueller
Library of Congress Catalog Card No. 72-83325
ISBN 0-916890-84-8

Published simultaneously in Canada by
Douglas & McIntyre Ltd.
1615 Venables St.
Vancouver B.C., V5L 2H1

Cover Photo: Portage Pass - Way No. 21
(Photo by Nancy Simmerman)
Title Photo: Monarch Peak in the Talkeetna Mountains—Way No. 48
(Photo by Gayle and Helen Nienhueser)

Hans van der Laan
November 17, 1937 - April 12, 1971

To Hans

Who still lives in the hearts of his family and friends and who, through his part in this book, shares with others his love of Alaska's mountains and valleys and his devotion to excellence.

"You cannot stay on the summit forever; you have to come down again. . . so why bother in the first place? Just this: what is above knows what is below, but what is below does not know what is above. One climbs, one sees. One descends, one sees no longer, but one has seen. There is an art of conducting oneself in the lower regions by the memory of what one saw higher up. When one can no longer see, one can at least still know."

From Rene Daumel's book, Mount Analogue, copyright 1959 by Pantheon Books, a Division of Random House, Inc.

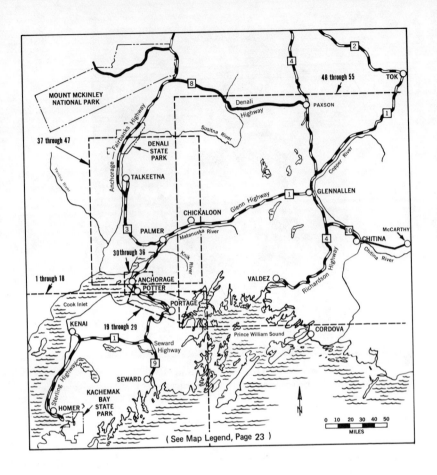

MOUNT MCKINLEY
NATIONAL PARK

2

4

48 through 55

TOK

Denali
Highway

PAXSON

1

37 through 47

Susitna River

DENALI
STATE
PARK

Copper River

Fairbanks Highway

Anchorage

TALKEETNA

Yentna River

CHICKALOON

Glenn Highway

1

GLENNALLEN

McCARTHY

3 PALMER

Matanuska River

4

10 CHITINA

30 through 36

Knik River

Chitina River

1 through 18

ANCHORAGE
POTTER

VALDEZ

Richardson Highway

Cook Inlet

PORTAGE

KENAI

19 through 29

Prince William Sound

CORDOVA

1

Seward
Highway

9

Sterling Highway

SEWARD

HOMER

KACHEMAK
BAY
STATE
PARK

N

0 10 20 30 40 50
MILES

(See Map Legend, Page 23)

TABLE OF CONTENTS

September morning, Alaska (Photo by Nancy Simmerman)

THE FUTURE OF ALASKA

Foreword

Why have we written this book? We have known and loved these mountains and valleys as wilderness and have found a special joy in walking here in solitude. We question our part in hastening a change by writing this book. Then why write it? Partly because we, too, were once newcomers here, once looked longingly at the mountains, but didn't know how to get there. So we know the need for a guide.

But more important, Alaska needs your help, whether you are a resident or a visitor. Alaska is indeed America's last great wilderness. If our book leads you into these mountains, and if you come to love them as we do, you too can help to keep them as they are.

Why? What is so important about Alaska? It is a symbol of wilderness, of freedom, of a way of life that is now only history in most of the United States. There was a wholesomeness, a directness, a satisfaction in that way of life, lived close to nature, that is missing from the lives of most Americans today. But because Alaska is there, and because Alaska still equals wilderness, there is hope. Hope that the values which made that way of life good may be rescued and made part of life again. Hope for each individual that he may someday experience Alaska wilderness firsthand.

What are the values derived from wilderness? Among the most important are simplicity and directness. In today's America we are divorced from our primary needs. Someone else produces our food, erects our shelter, protects us from the harsher elements of nature. When we live in the wilderness, even for a weekend backpacking trip, we grapple once again with some of the basic problems, and we are dependent on ourselves alone for the solutions.

Wilderness is also beauty, peace, harmony, silence. A source of strength. The opportunity, not to conquer nature, but to test oneself against the elements and to gain mastery over oneself. The opportunity to know ourselves and others away from the distractions of civilization. And more: aliveness, spontaneity, affirmation—qualities which make life more than mere existence. The further we go away from wilderness living, the dimmer these values become. Without wilderness as a source of renewal, how long can we sustain them?

The simple existence of wilderness in the world is enough. Not everyone need go there. It remains a symbol for those who do not go, a direct source of renewal for those who do. Indirectly the lives of all will be enriched because wilderness exists.

What are the Chances?

What are the chances of preserving a good percentage of Alaska's wilderness? That depends on the public. Among many Alaskans there is a strong and sincere feeling that they have the right to see their state develop as other states have and that each individual should have the opportunity to make money from the development. This is the frontier philosophy and has been a strong American tradition. There has been, however, a tremendous change in attitudes in Alaska in the last few years. The conservation movement has taken hold and is growing in strength. Although conservation and preservation are bad words to some, many others are beginning to see that times have changed, that there is no more wilderness beyond Alaska, and that Alaska's development must not and need not follow the pattern of other states. In these changing attitudes there is real hope.

Alaska became a state in 1959. During the first ten years of statehood little was done by the state to protect its lands for future uses. In the early 70's the legislature created Chugach State Park, Denali State Park, Kachemak Bay State Park and Chilkat State Park. Various state recreation areas and state game refuges have also been established.

In 1978 Wood-Tikchik State Park (north of Dillingham) was established. Two other important proposals were left pending: the Hatcher Pass State Recreation Area (Trips 44, 45, 46) and Keystone Canyon State Park (north of Valdez). These will need continued support to achieve passage. A number of legislators erroneously believe that the federal government's interest in creating national parks in Alaska relieves them of a similar responsibility on state lands. They fail to realize that the national proposals are generally remote from population centers and designed primarily for visitors from the lower 48 states. The State still has the responsibility of providing for the recreational needs of its citizens in areas which are easily accessible.

More Needs to be Done

Some steps have been taken in the right direction, but more needs to be done. Of course not all of Alaska can be kept as parkland, but large and representative samples of the state can and should be preserved as wilderness. Other parts must be developed for recreational use. Enough must be set aside in these ways to retain quality in the outdoor experience. Tourist use of Alaska's parks and recreation areas will increase; we must have more to offer than a few overcrowded Yosemites. Alaska's wilderness is a national asset, belonging to all Americans, present and future, and deserves recognition as such. It must be remembered that at present the federal government (i.e., all Americans) owns about 95 per cent of Alaska's land and that even after state selection and settlement of the Native land claims the federal government will still own at least 60 per cent of the state. Alaska is rightfully the heritage of all 50 states.

Alaska is at a crossroads. The state has the opportunity now to affect the direction of its future, the extent and quality of its growth. As part of the opportunity, the state has the option of approving the pending state park proposals and establishing others. The federal government has the opportunity of establishing Wilderness Areas in Alaska under the Wilderness Act of 1964 and of adding new lands to the National Park, Forest, Wildlife Refuge, and Wild and Scenic River Systems under the Alaska Native Claims Settlement Act of 1971.

We Need Your Help

As you have read, Alaska is threatened. Vocal concern on the part of Alaska's residents and friends is necessary. Make your views known to those in power through letters and public hearings. Politicians are sensitive to public opinion, and politicians and agencies are responsive to it. Join or support one or all of the Alaskan and national conservation groups listed on page 164.

Helen Nienhueser
revised June, 1978

Raven Glacier near Crow Pass – Way No. 25 (Photo by Nancy Simmerman)

HIKING IN ALASKA

This book is a guide to routes and trails that take the hiker into some of Alaska's wild and beautiful backcountry. Trip suggestions were compiled from many sources and then investigated; we hope the results will include a few new trips even for the most experienced Alaskan hikers.

Hiking in Alaska is different from hiking in the more developed parts of the United States. Here we have few trails; many of the trips described are simply routes. Some of the trails we do have are not marked or maintained. Some of the access roads were privately built and are not maintained; few are marked.

Each trip was checked by Nancy Simmerman or Helen Nienhueser and directions carefully noted. But because so many routes and roads are not marked, we relied on mileages for our directions. The Alaskan highways are marked with mileposts every mile; where possible we used these mileposts in giving directions. In some cases the mileposts were not standing, and car odometers were used to calculate the distance from the nearest milepost. (They were also used on side-roads.) There can be considerable variation among cars in registering mileage, which may result in some discrepancy between mileages given here and as registered on your car.

Glenn Highway (Alaska Route 1) mileposts begin in Anchorage; Parks Highway (Alaska Route 3) mileposts begin in Anchorage; Richardson Highway (Alaska Route 4) mileposts in Valdez; Seward Highway (Alaska Routes 1 and 9) in Seward. The Sterling Highway (Alaska Route 1) mileposts also begin in Seward and coincide with the Seward Highway mileposts for the first 37½ miles.

When a road does not receive public maintenance its condition varies greatly from year to year; there is no guarantee it will be driveable. If there are doubts about whether your car can make it, don't try it. Getting a tow truck may take hours and be very expensive, and residents have become weary of pulling people out. Furthermore, driving a road when it is muddy tears it up, which is unfair to the residents who maintain it themselves.

Trails, too, present a problem; when not marked or maintained the hiker is likely to wonder whether he is on the right trail, despite directions and maps. On both roads and trails, learn to trust your instinct for the right fork, and keep your sense of humor if you take the wrong fork. Retrace your steps and start over. When there is a network of unmarked trails and roads which may change annually, as is true of several hikes described here, it is impossible to write infallible directions.

A word of cheer for those who prefer paved roads and well-marked trails — we have some! Most are on the Kenai Peninsula where U.S. Forest Service and Kenai Moose Range personnel are continually developing trails that start from the highway system.

It was sometimes difficult to pick the time of year when each trip is "best"; snow conditions vary considerably from year to year. For this reason we cannot say when in June a given route will open. Hiking is usually good through September and elevations below 4000 feet may be snow-free well into October.

May is a tricky month in Alaska. At the lower elevations it is summer, but above 2500 to 3000 feet it is still winter. For trips above these elevations take winter equipment. An easy climb in summer may call for a rope under winter conditions.

Hiking time given is for an average adult hiker taking occasional short rest stops; some will be faster and some slower, especially families. Hiking time without a trail, particularly if climbing, may be 1 mile per hour; on a good trail, hiking time should be at least 2 miles per hour.

A few terms used in the book need definition. **Timberline** refers to the area on a mountain beyond which trees do not grow. Beyond the trees is brush. Alder, that

Turnagain Pass ski route, December –Way No. 18 (Photo by Nancy Simmerman)

tree-like shrub which can create an almost impenetrable tangle, is classified as brush. **Brushline** is the area on a mountain beyond which brush, including alder, does not grow. **Tundra** is used to describe a type of vegetation which grows above brushline. **Taiga** refers to the forested areas of subarctic lands.

Equipment

A good guide to equipment and hiking and camping know-how is **Mountaineering: The Freedom of the Hills,** by The Mountaineers, Seattle, Washington. In it The Mountaineers list ten essentials to be carried at all times: (1) extra clothing; (2) extra food; (3) sunglasses; (4) knife; (5) matches; (6) firestarter (e.g., candle); (7) first aid kit (leave the snakebite kit home); (8) flashlight (except in June and July); (9) map; (10) compass.

Even for a day trip, a small backpack is convenient for carrying the extra clothing and lunch. For overnights use a pack with a frame, one that carries the weight high, rather than a rucksack. Hiking cross-country is easier if wearing good hiking boots with rubber lug soles. Leather boots can be waterproofed by rubbing a silicone preparation into them. To reduce the chance of blisters, wear one heavy pair of wool socks with a lightweight rayon or nylon pair underneath next to the skin. Carry a roll of paper adhesive tape, and tape any rub spots when you first notice them, not after a blister has formed. Many Alaskan hikers routinely carry a lightweight rain poncho, a waterproof jacket, or a large plastic garbage bag for protection from an unexpected rain shower.

Winter trips require additional equipment. A heavy down or dacron parka with windproof hood is desirable and almost mandatory on overnight trips. Loose-fitting layers are warmest. For wet snow, snowshoers should wear one of the following: insulated rubber "Korean" boots; waterproof shoepacs with a change of felt liners in the backpack; a hiking boot with insulated overboot. For cold snow (below 15°F) canvas or fur mukluks are good. Check the surplus stores for footgear.

Skiers on overnight trips will be better off with a double boot or insulated overboots over the regular ski touring boot. Take lightweight mukluks or down or dacron slippers (to wear under the overboots) for in-camp use.

Necessary for all winter travel are: leather mittens with heavy wool liners plus an extra pair of liners; extra wool socks; long johns under wool pants or skiers' insulated warm-up pants without zippers; a wool hat; a face mask. Wool or dacron is stressed because it is warm even when wet. Gaiters, worn over pants bottom and boot top, keep the snow out. To avoid condensation, clothing should not be waterproof for winter trips. If you expect to encounter temperatures near freezing, take rain gear, too.

Snowshoes will travel up and downhill more easily if the wooden frame is wrapped with heavy nylon cord to provide greater traction. The toe of the boot should be able to move freely in the toe opening; if the foot slides forward to cover the opening, tighten the bindings. We suggest the long narrow trail snowshoes (Alaskan model, 10" x 56").

For cross-country ski touring it is necessary to have bindings which allow the heel to lift. Some downhill bindings can be used with an attachment which allows the heel to come up but the units are heavy. Ski mountaineers generally use downhill skis with a touring attachment and use climbing skins on their skis for uphill. For skiing over flat or rolling terrain, touring equipment is preferable. The skis are wood or fiberglass, lighter weight, and have bottoms to which climbing wax can be applied, making climbing skins unnecessary except for steep slopes. "No wax" skis are excellent for the changing snow conditions found on spring ski tours. The boots are light and flexible, and the lightweight binding permits maximum heel lift.

Additional information on winter equipment and travel can be found in the Sierra Club paperback, **Manual of Ski Mountaineering,** edited by David Brower.

Portaging canoes and kayaks is much more comfortable if a sturdy 2 x 4, longer than the width of the boat, is lashed across the top of a pack frame. The gunnels of the overturned boat rest on the 2 x 4.

Precautions

HYPOTHERMIA: Winter conditions are never far away in Alaska, even in midsummer. Hikers and skiers should go prepared with extra warm clothing and high calorie snack foods. Excessive loss of body core heat can result in hypothermia, often called "exposure," in which the metabolic and physiological processes of the body are slowed. Death can result if body heat continues to be lost.

Cold weather (even above 32°F), wetness (rain or perspiration), wind, and the hiker's exhaustion or poor conditioning impose a stress on the cardiovascular system. When the body can no longer meet its heat and energy needs, hypothermia begins. The problem is compounded at high altitudes.

Progressive Symptoms of Hypothermia
(Adapted from "Hypothermia," Chugach State Park publication.)

Body Temperature (°F)	Symptom
97 - 96	Uncontrollable shivering, slowing of rate of progress.
95 - 91	Slurred speech, sluggish thinking, forgetfulness, clumsiness.
90 - 86	Shivering slowly decreases, muscles become rigid and cramped, reluctance to continue.
85 - 81	Victim becomes irrational, may be unable to continue.

80 - 78   Unconsciousness.
Below 78   Usually results in death.

Treatment of Hypothermia
1. Move victim out of wind and rain, even if it means forcing him to the nearest available shelter.
2. Get victim out of wet clothing.
3. Place victim in a sleeping bag or blankets and, if necessary, remove your own clothing and get into the sleeping bag with the victim. Your body will warm his.
4. Get food and/or warm liquids into victim. The heat produced by food is limited by the type - carbohydrates produce heat the fastest; proteins take about 45 minutes to produce heat; fats take 5-8 hours. Do not give victims alcohol!

Avoid Hypothermia through prevention
1. Dress for warmth, against both wind and rain.
2. Take extra dry clothing.
3. Protect head and hands - up to 40% of your body heat can be lost through the head.
4. Carry emergency gear - buy or put together your own survival kit.
5. Eat and drink - keep up a continuous intake of high-energy foods such as sweets while on the trail. Avoid dehydration. When chilled, do not eat snow; it lowers body temperature.
6. Keep active.

Weather changeability is the rule in Alaska. Be prepared - and enjoy a safe trip.

FIRE: In dry years, Alaska is subject to disastrous forest fires. Because of the slow decay rate the soil (peat) underneath the surface may burn, spreading a campfire underground. Throughout the 1969-70 winter about 16 fires smouldered under-ground. For this reason it is important to build fires carefully; build small fires only on mineral soil. If a gravel or bare dirt surface is not available dig far enough down through the peat to reach solid dirt or gravel. Face the exposed peat with rocks. Be sure to have water available to put the fire out, and make certain every spark is out before leaving. The infallible test is to touch the ashes with bare hands. Check the underside of any partially burned logs. Before leaving, wet thoroughly the peat within a foot of the fire area. Where possible, build on top of old campfires to avoid unnecessary scars; use only dead trees for fuel. No open fires are permitted in Chugach State Park. Chugach National Forest and the Kenai Moose Range may announce bans on open fires during dry seasons.

PLANTS: Although Alaska is free of poison ivy and poison oak, it does have a few plants which should be avoided. These include stinging nettle, devil's club, bane-berry, and poisonous mushrooms. The Federal Extension Service sells pamphlets on **Wild Edible and Poisonous Plants of Alaska** and **Know Alaska's Mushrooms**. It is located on the University of Alaska campus in Anchorage; the mailing address is 2651 Providence Ave., Anchorage, 99504. Other books on Alaska's plants and mushrooms are available at local bookstores.

MOOSE AND BEARS: Also better avoided are moose and bears. Normally a moose will run from a hiker, but a cow moose with a calf can be dangerous, and wherever there is a calf, a cow moose is nearby. Stopping to take a picture is not recommended. Experienced Alaskan outdoorsmen recommend against taking an unleashed dog into the wilds because the dog may go after a moose or a bear and end up being chased right back to his master.

Black bears, the kind most likely to be found near Anchorage, generally head away from man. Brown or grizzly bears, found on the Kenai Peninsula and north and east of Anchorage, are more dangerous, but rarely attack without provocation. Many Alaskans carry a gun, and the U.S. Forest Service encourages those traveling in brown bear country to carry a 30-06 or larger rifle. Those hikers unwilling to carry a gun should make a lot of noise, especially in deep brush where it is possible to come upon a bear suddenly. Popular noisemakers are bells tied to the pack, waist, or boots; pebbles in a canteen; loud singing or whistling; beating on a pot with a spoon; a whistle. Before going to bed, wash your hands and face carefully and brush teeth to remove food odors. Do not keep food in your tent at night. Cache it in a tree or in your pack **outside** the tent. Keep all food wrapped tightly in plastic bags; do not carry bacon or peanut butter. Mothballs in small net bags, attached to food bags, discourage animal raiders when no trees are available to hang caches.

Care should be taken to avoid bears, but what to do if an encounter occurs? Will Troyer, a biologist with the National Park Service in Alaska, who has had considerable experience with bears, says: "If possible approach bears upwind so they get your scent. This usually sends them in the other direction. But no two bears are alike. Though unlikely, you may run into a grumpy old male, or a cross female that is very protective of her cubs. If you do find yourself face to face with such a bear, take evasive action. Start talking in a loud voice, shout if necessary, and slowly back off. By all means **do not turn and run;** this only invites a chase. If a tree or rock outcropping is nearby, climb it. Jumping in a stream or lake often stops an advancing bear. If the bear continues to approach, yell louder or wave your arms. Firecrackers are excellent deterrents. Another good deterrent is throwing your hat toward the bear. Many times the odor from the hat will do the trick; if not, the bear may stop to investigate the hat, giving you time to climb a tree. If all this fails, and you have met the one bear in a thousand that means harm, lie on your stomach, preferably in a depression, with your hands over your head. Keep your pack on, because a protruding pack is often what the bear will bite."

STREAM CROSSINGS: A few of the hikes described include crossing potentially hazardous streams. To cross such a stream safely: (1) look for the widest part of the stream where the water will be shallowest and least swift; (2) wear boots to insure good footing (if socks are taken off and kept dry until the other side, walking in wet boots will not be uncomfortable); or (3) carry tennis shoes for crossing—not as good in really fast, deep streams; (4) undo the waist strap of the pack for ease in getting it off should a fall occur; (5) put the camera inside the pack in a waterproof sack, or its strap may make removal of a pack impossible; (6) for very swift water take along a rope and belay each person as he crosses; (7) use a stick or ice axe to probe for safe footing and for additional support. In swifter streams such as Eagle River, do not use a stick. Hold hands with each other for stability; (8) point toes downstream and walk diagonally, with the current; (9) plan the trip in early summer or a crossing for the early morning when water levels are likely to be lower; (10) lightweight or small people should add rocks to the backpack for more weight, providing more secure footing.

Large braided streams may be crossed more easily if the hiker takes advantage of the stream's natural flow pattern. Scout the river from a vantage point to find an area with many channels. Cross from the upstream end of one gravel island to the upstream end of the next. Here the water is shallower and slower due to gravel deposition by nearby channels. Just below this point the water is swifter and deeper. The downstream end of a gravel island where channels converge may hide a deep turbulent hole or soft sand. For more information about crossing streams, see **Mountaineering: Freedom of the Hills.**

LITTER: All garbage and litter should be carried home. Burying it is not acceptable. It will usually be dug up by animals, and it invites bears to investigate the campsite, thus

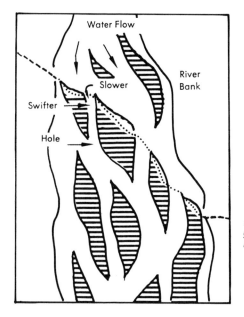

A braided stream showing gravel islands and a suggested route for crossing the stream

endangering the next camper. Garbage pits are also unnecessary scars upon the landscape. Carry a heavy-duty plastic bag for carrying out empty cans and garbage. This includes soiled toilet paper; it can be carried in a plastic bag and burned later if convenient. The only exception is disposal of used tampons in bear country; burn if possible; if not, bury immediately and never near camp. Take care to toilet some distance away from streams and lakes, and thus avoid contaminating them.

MOSQUITOES: Though not as much of a problem in southcentral Alaska as in the Interior, mosquitoes are annoying to many people. Everyone carries repellent, and those who are particularly sensitive carry head nets.

AVALANCHES: If you travel in the mountains in the winter or spring on foot, by skis, snowshoes, doglsed, snowmachine, or automobile, know about avalanches. Avalanche deaths have increased in recent years in southcentral Alaska as more people travel off the beaten trail. Educate yourself and have a safe trip. Call the Chugach State Park office for information concerning avalanche courses which are held for the public each winter in the Anchorage area. Meanwhile, study thoroughly **The ABC of Avalanche Safety** by Ed LaChapelle and the sections on avalanches in **Manual of Ski Mountaineering** edited by David Brower and in **Mountaineering: The Freedom of the Hills.**

Before you go into the backcountry, find out about the current avalanche conditions by calling one of the following numbers:

Chugach National Forest: 274-4113 (recording), 272-4485 (other information); Chugach State Park: 274-6713 (recording), 279-3413 (other information); Southcentral Alaska Recreational Weather Forecast: 936-2727 (recording).

Avalanche: avoid and survive (from "Avalanche!", Chugach State Park publication)
Terrain field notes
• Avalanches are most common on slopes of 30 to 45 degrees.
• Slab avalanches are more apt to occur on convex slopes, or at the brow of a hill.
• In midwinter there is greater danger on north-facing slopes.

Typical avalanche path down timbered mountainside. Upper mountain below ridge top (starting zone), blaze (track and runout zone), and nearby trees should be considered potentially hazardous in winter and spring. Although timbered slopes define avalanche zones, be alert for similar zones in treeless areas. (Clearings to right are natural.)

- On south-facing slopes the danger increases on sunny days and in spring.
- Leeward slopes tend to collect snow in cornices and other forms. They are more dangerous because of this.
- Windward of a crest may be safer because of compacted snow or less snow.
- Any hill that is open, without rocks, trees, or heavy vegetation to anchor the snow, presents a greater hazard.

Weather field notes

- Wind over 15 mph can increase the danger as it moves snow onto leeward slopes. Look above for plumes rising from peaks and ridges.
- The time of greatest avalanche activity is during or immediately following a storm; 80% of all slides occur at this time.
- The faster snow falls beyond one inch per hour, the faster danger increases.
- Snow that has already lost the six-armed star shape as it comes to the ground is more of a problem.
- Temperature near or above freezing tends to settle the pack.
- Continued cold weather can cause snow to persist in an unstable condition.

It is unfortunate but true that the conditions skiers love so much — a new storm deposit, at least a foot of light and fluffy snow, and an open slope with a 30 to 45 degree pitch, are just the conditions preferred by avalanches. That is why ski-lift areas are so busy blasting and grooming their trails. None of these services exist outback, so cross-country skiers in the wilderness must use extra caution.

Route selection and observation

• Contact the local authority, ski patrol, or ranger — someone with information on local conditions.

• Pack and use avalanche cords — electronic transceivers are better — and a sectional probe.

• Use routes on ridge tops, to the windward side. Next best is on the valley flat, well away from runout areas.

• Watch for old avalanche blaze marks: fracture lines above, debris below, a lack of large trees in between.

• Avoid gullies.

• Watch for running cracks.

• Listen for hollow sounds.

If you must travel on a dangerous slope —

• Do not traverse the hill; take a straight up or down route.

• Only one person at a time, with all equipment loosened, should go ahead. All others should watch and wait.

• Stay as near the top as possible if you must cross a slope.

• Use dense woods or rocky ridges as islands of safety.

If you are caught —

• Get rid of any equipment you can. Skis, for example, can pinion you more firmly.

• Make a vigorous effort to swim, trying to move toward the top and the side of the flow.

• Try to keep snow from packing into your mouth. If you can tell that things are slowing down, try to get an arm in front of your face to form an air space.

• Stay calm to conserve air and strength.

If you have just seen someone swept away —

• Mark the spot where the person was last seen. Search directly downhill of the marked spot.

• If you are the only person at the scene, do not leave immediately to go for help, unless it is very close by.

• If there is more than one remaining in a party, one should leave to find aid, the others organize a probe line to work methodically across the debris.

• Remember, after one hour the buried have only a 50% survival rate.

For U.S. Forest Service information, write to: The Rocky Mountain Forest and Range Experiment Station, 240 West Prospect Avenue, Fort Collins, CO 80521.

SAFETY: Deaths have occurred along the routes of some of these hikes. By long experience The Mountaineers have devised a climbing code which in large part applies to hikers, too. If followed, potential disaster can be avoided.

A climbing party of three is the minimum, unless adequate prearranged support is available. . .

Carry at all times the clothing, food, and equipment necessary.

Rope up on all exposed places. . .

Keep the party together and obey the leader or majority rule.

Never climb beyond your ability and knowledge.

Never let judgment be swayed by desire when choosing the route or turning back.

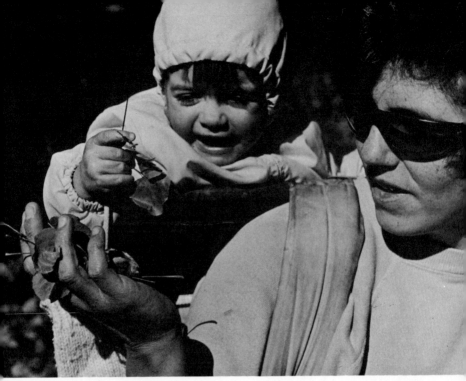

Young children are easily carried in a specially designed commercially available backpack. (Photo by Nancy Simmerman)

Leave the trip schedule with a responsible person.

Follow the precepts of sound mountaineering as set forth in **Mountaineering: The Freedom of the Hills** and other textbooks of recognized merit.

Behave at all times in a manner that will not reflect unfavorably upon. . . mountaineering.

Hiking With Children

What hikes are good for children? That depends on the child, his age, experience, and attitude. Experienced Alaskan hikers take their children on almost all these trips, but some are certainly too long or difficult for the average child. Try your children on the easier trips first. Babies can go most anywhere in a kiddy pack; a 3-year-old should be able to manage several miles a day with an occasional piggyback ride; children of 5 and up can easily cover 4 to 5 miles a day, and often more. Pick a trip that is interesting to the child, that has a stream or lake to play in or rocks to climb on. A long, steep climb with no diversions is boring for children. Carry water and favorite nibble food always, plus a small toy or two. See page 162 for suggested trips.

Where to Get More Information

Many of the trips described here are in the Kenai National Moose Range, Chugach National Forest, and Chugach State Park. Insofar as known, the plans for changes in trails have been included in the text, but up-to-date information can be obtained from the agencies. The Forest Service maintains a number of cabins for public use. These are popular and reservations must be made well in advance through any of the

Chugach National Forest offices listed below. A fee is charged for reserving the cabins and use of the campgrounds.

Each agency has its own regulations. In the Chugach National Forest and the Kenai National Moose Range, fire building and camping are not restricted, although fire building outside established campgrounds may be prohibited during times of high fire hazard. Chugach State Park prohibits open fires at all times.   Part of Chugach State Park is also Anchorage watershed.

The Chugach State Park encourages backcountry travellers to file a trip plan with the Anchorage office for their own safety. (Phone: 279-3413.)

Further information can be obtained from:

Refuge Manager, Kenai National Moose Range
Box 500, Kenai, Alaska 99611

U.S. Forest Service
Chugach National Forest
2221 E. Northern Lights Blvd., Room 101,
Anchorage, Alaska 99504
For information: 279-5541
For cabin reservations: 345-2519 (Anchorage)
  Box 275, Seward 99664 (224-3023)
  Box 280, Cordova 99574 (424-7661)
For avalanche and recreation recordings: 271-4500 and 274-4113.

Chugach State Park
2601 Commercial Drive
Anchorage, Alaska 99501
For avalanche and recreation recordings: 271-4500 and 274-4113.
For other information or to file trip plan: 279-3413.

ACKNOWLEDGMENTS

This book follows in the footsteps of **30 Hikes in Alaska,** written by members of the Mountaineering Club of Alaska, edited by William E. Hauser, and published by The Mountaineers in 1967. A few of the trips in **30 Hikes** have been deleted because of access or other problems, but most of the original trips have been included in this edition. Although each trip was rechecked to insure current information, there are a number of instances in which the original description has been retained. Those who contributed to **30 Hikes** were Robert Spurr, Hans van der Laan, John Wolfe, J. Vincent Hoeman, Nicholas Parker, Carol and David DeVoe, Gary Hansen, Rodman and Gwynneth Wilson, William Hague, Ron Linder, and Helen Nienhueser.

The first edition has been helped along by many. First on the list of those to whom thanks are due is husband Gayle Nienhueser, without whose patience this book would not exist. Special thanks are due to Liska Snyder for editorial assistance and Doris Curtis for typing.

We wish particularly to thank the many agencies and their representatives who helped us time and again with information: officials of the Alaska Department of Fish and Game, especially Jay Bergstrand, for making available their field notes on trails, and James Hemming; officials of the Bureau of Sport Fisheries and Wildlife, especially Willard Troyer, David Spencer, and John Kurtz; officials of the U.S. Forest Service, especially Charles O'Leary, Richard Woodrow, and Kenneth Rikard; officials of the Alaska Division of Parks, especially Theodore Smith, Richard Alman, Neil Johannsen, and William Hanable; officials of the Bureau of Land Management, especially Wayne Boden; Dave Skitt of the Anchorage Water Utility Division; officials of the Geological Survey; Bruce Freitag of the Alaska Department of Highways.

Other Mountaineering Club of Alaska members and mountaineers who were a great help in preparation of the book are: Dona Agosti, Joanne Barnes, Winford C. Bludworth, Jr., Paul Crews, Dayton Curtis, Carol and David DeVoe, Christopher Friedrichs, Nat Goodhue, Steve Hackett, Paul Hansen, Elizabeth Hatton, David Henney, Grace Hoeman, John and Betty Ireton, Catherine Kippenhan, Lois Lindemood, Marie Lundstrom, George Mark, Joanne and John Merrick, John Samuelson, Ruth Schmidt, Charles Simmerman, Dick Snyder, William Stivers, Barbara Wilson, Rodman Wilson and John Wolfe. We wish space permitted us to list the many others who also helped, chiefly by answering endless questions. Without them many useful bits of information would be missing from the book.

Grateful appreciation also to Justin Stauter, who helped with historical background, Locke Jacobs who furnished us with copying facilities, Mark Ganopole, Sam Wright, and Walter Parker who reviewed the foreword, and to the Literary Fund Committee of The Mountaineers, most especially the committee's "North Editor," E. Allen Robinson, our constant companion in this effort, and Tom Miller, Harvey Manning, and other Mountaineers who helped guide the book through the final production stage.

And to all readers who do their part, however small, in keeping these areas of Alaska unchanged, our heartfelt thanks.

Helen Nienhueser
Nancy Simmerman
Hans van der Laan

Acknowledgments to the Second Edition:

Neil Johannsen and Sandy Rabinowitz, Alaska State Parks; Doug Fesler, Ellen Hambleton, Dale Bingham, and Mike Rodak, Chugach State Park; Louise Bremner, Alaska Railroad; Edward Bennett, Michael Polzin, David Finklestein, Dick Hensil, Mark Hickok, Sally Gibert, and David Levine. Again our thanks to Al Robinson, our liaison with The Mountaineers in Seattle, who was enticed to move to Alaska through his work on this book.

Helen Nienhueser
Nancy Simmerman

AN INVITATION

The Mountaineers

The Mountaineers, with groups based in Seattle, Everett, Tacoma, and Olympia, warmly invite membership of all lovers of outdoor life who sympathize with the purposes of the organization and wish to share its activities.

The Mountaineers sponsor a year-around program of climbing, hiking, camping, ski-touring, snowshoeing, canoeing and kayaking, and bicycling. Many hundreds of outings are scheduled each year, ranging from afternoon walks to trips lasting 2 weeks or more. On a typical weekend as many as 50 excursions may be offered, from ocean beaches to the summit of Mount Rainier. In addition, members engage in countless privately-organized trips of all kinds; the opportunity is boundless to make new friends with similar interests.

Enjoying wildlands is one side of the coin; the other is working to preserve the natural beauty of Northwest America. Here, The Mountaineers continue their role of leadership as they have for over 70 years, and seek new members to share the effort.

For membership application, and further information on club activities, write The Mountaineers, 719 Pike St., Seattle, Washington 98101.

The Mountaineering Club of Alaska

The Mountaineering Club of Alaska is a group of hikers and climbers who gather to exchange information about Alaskan climbing and hiking, plan trips, construct refuge cabins in the glacial wilderness, instruct beginners in the joys and responsibilities of mountaineering, and help in keeping the mountain world enjoyable. To join, write P.O. Box 2037, Anchorage, Alaska. Meetings are held monthly and a newsletter, **Scree,** is published monthly.

Though all information contained in this book has been carefully checked, some errors no doubt exist. In some cases information will be soon outdated as highway and trail development takes place. Corrections and suggestions should be sent to the authors in care of the Mountaineering Club of Alaska.

MAPS

Trip maps are all made by superimposing additional information onto portions of United States Geological Survey (USGS) maps. Scale and north orientation vary between maps so the scale and north arrow on each map should be noted.

Prior to making any but the shortest trips the hiker should obtain a copy of the appropriate USGS map as noted with each trip description. If the hiker should stray from the indicated route it is possible to go off the section of map shown in this book and become lost. Also, geographic features which are useful for routefinding may lie off the section of map shown and the entire map, and perhaps the adjacent one also, will be needed to identify such features. Scrutinizing the entire USGS map will often suggest other trips not described in this book.

Some trails shown in this book differ from those shown on the USGS map. In those cases field investigation has shown the USGS map to be outdated, as some trails on the USGS maps no longer exist.

USGS maps may be obtained in Anchorage from the U.S. Geological Survey Office, 508 W. 2nd Ave., or by mail from the USGS, Federal Center, Denver, Colorado 80202. Their cost is small, and their worth immeasurable.

LEGEND

Start of Trip	●	City or Town	○
Trail		Boundary	
Route		Powerline	
Paved Road	8	Trip Number or Point of Interest	⑳
Gravel Road			
Marginal Road		Bridge	≍
Railroad		Building	■

Opposite: false hellebore, upper Winner Creek, July. Top: left, bunchberry or ground dogwood, July; right, blueberries, September. Below: left, Amanita muscaria, a poisonous mushroom, September; right, fern, September. (Photos by Nancy Simmerman)

U.S. Forest Service cabin on Crescent Lake (Photo by Nancy Simmerman)

The U.S. Forest Service maintains wilderness cabins for the use of hikers and skiers. Available for a nominal charge and by reservation only, the cabins contain a stove for cooking and heating, miscellaneous cooking utensils, and bunks. Frequently, cabins situated on a lake will have a rowboat for the use of rentees. Contact the Anchorage office of the U.S. Forest Service for reservations and further information. Hikes with cabins are: No. 8, Upper Russian Lake; No. 9, Crescent Lake; No. 14, Resurrection Pass system; and No. 25, Crow Pass.

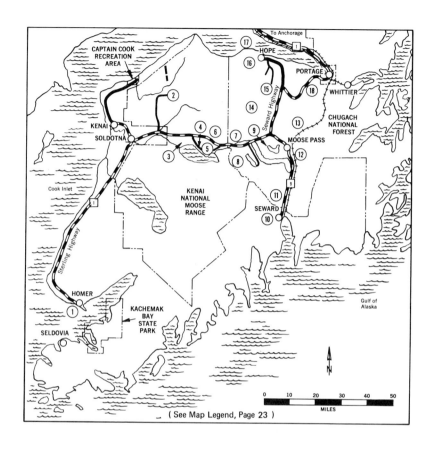

(See Map Legend, Page 23)

KENAI PENINSULA

KENAI PENINSULA

1 Homer Beach Walk

Round trip 4 miles
Hiking time 5-6 hours
High point sea level
Elevation gain none
Best anytime
USGS map Seldovia C5

A delightfully different Alaskan experience which still boasts of superb mountain scenery. Homer and Kachemak Bay can be classified as one of Alaska's loveliest areas. The beach walk takes the hiker away from civilization and at low tide he will find starfish, various kinds of clam shells, mussels (some alive and clinging to rocks in great profusion), whelk (neptune) shells, rocks covered with barnacles, sea urchins, snails, crabs, seagulls, kittiwakes, and other small shore birds. Coal and sometimes fossils can be found below the cliffs which border the beach. Waterfalls cascade down

Beach at Homer, May. (Photo by Gayle and Helen Nienhueser)

the cliffs, driftwood can be found almost any time, and there is always the panoramic mountain view across the bay. Excellent for children of all ages.

At low tide there is a broad sandy beach but at high tide the sand is covered and the hiker is walking on gravel. Be sure to consult tide tables, available from most gas stations and banks, before leaving. Pick a day with a reasonably low tide, and schedule the walk to leave before low tide and return to Homer well before high tide. At times the tide comes in all the way to the cliffs. This poses a potential hazard, as in some places the cliffs cannot be climbed and one could conceivably be trapped in rising water. However, there is no danger if one watches the hour. To keep feet dry wear rubber boots or well-greased hiking boots, as there are many little inlets left behind by the retreating water which must be crossed. Take care not to be trapped on a little island as the tide pours back into these inlets, turning peninsulas into islands and cutting off retreat.

At the bottom of the hill entering Homer, where the paved road goes left into town, a gravel road (opposite the Homer School) goes straight ahead to the beach. Follow this road and park at the end on the right, on a small bluff overlooking the beach.

A trail leads to the beach. Wander up the beach to your right (west) as far as desired, as long as there is enough time to get back before high tide. A good destination is a rocky spit about 2 miles down the beach which extends far out into the water at low tide and offers excellent beachcombing. Shortly after low tide this spit is totally covered by water so time the walk to be there at low tide (close to an hour of steady walking—much longer if you beachcomb en route).

At very low tide there is also good beachcombing available on the east side of the base of Homer Spit at Mud Bay.

Homer has a nice campground on the hill above town. Directions to it are posted on signs by the road into town.

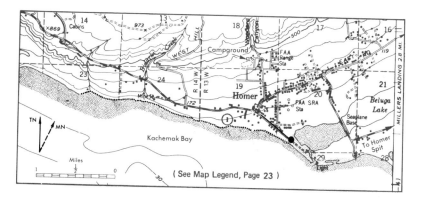

(See Map Legend, Page 23)

KENAI PENINSULA

2 Swan Lake and Swanson River Canoe Routes

Swan Lake: one-way trip up to 60 miles
Allow 2 days to 1 week
Gradient 4 feet per mile
Best May—early October
USGS map Kenai C2

Swanson River: up to 80 miles
2 days to 1 week
Gradient 4 feet per mile
Best late May—early October
USGS maps Kenai D1, D2, D3, C2, C3
Kenai National Moose Range

This chain of lakes, streams, and rivers through wooded northwestern Kenai Peninsula offers good safe canoeing and kayaking. Rough water is seldom a problem as the lakes are small and the rivers placid. Portages are short, well-marked, and well-cleared. Take 2 days or 2 weeks — many route variations are possible. A rich variety of water birds inhabit these lakes and streams, including ducks, loons, snipes, swans, and yellow legs. The fisherman will find rainbow trout, Dolly Varden, steelhead trout, and landlocked salmon. Watch for moose, beaver, muskrat, and bear. The canoe trails offer potential for good cross-country ski tours in winter.

The Swan Lake and Swanson River Canoe Routes are two separate systems. Both are reached by traveling on the Sterling Highway to about mile 84, 1⅓ miles west of the Moose River bridge. Here turn north on well-marked Robinson Loop Road (which runs into Swanson River Road). No gas beyond here. Turn east off this road onto Swan Lake Road (marked) about 17 miles from the Sterling Highway. Swan Lake Canoe Route lies south of Swan Lake Road, and Swanson River Canoe Route lies north.

The west entrance to Swan Lake Canoe Route is in about 4 miles; the east entrance is 6 miles farther. From either entrance the canoeist can reach Moose River, which he can follow to the bridge on the Sterling Highway. This trip can be done in 2 long, hard days, but more time is recommended. It takes nearly a day to reach Gavia Lake from either entrance, several hours from there to Swan Lake, and at least 6 hours to reach Moose River bridge from Swan Lake. Time will vary according to experience and efficiency at handling portages. Camping along the Moose River during the first 1½ hours is poor. An easier 2-day trip is from one entrance to the other via Gavia Lake. Many other variations are possible.

The Swanson River Canoe Route entrance is about 2 miles beyond Swan Lake east entrance. A road leads north to Paddle Lake. From there enjoy various routes among the lakes, or take a 2-day trip through several lakes and out Swanson River. To do this head north from Paddle Lake to Gene Lake (1 day), then down Swanson River to Swanson River Road (1 long day). More time is more fun. In dry years check ahead with the Refuge Manager, Kenai Moose Range, Box 500, Kenai, Alaska, 99611. Low water can make several miles of the Swanson River impassable. The small stream connecting Gene Lake and Swanson River generally requires lining the boat and includes two short portages. Most campsites along the river are some distances back from shore. A campsite can be found at the end of the second portage between Gene Lake and the river. Canoeists can also follow Swanson River to its mouth.

Good primitive campsites are available on both routes. Campfires may be restricted in dry years. Although firewood is available, take a small stove as most

Swan Lake-Swanson River canoe route (Photo by Nancy
Simmerman)

campsites are on peat or moss which will burn and where it is therefore dangerous to build fires. Build a small fire, only on bare rock or soil, and be sure every spark is out before leaving. The 1969 fire in this area was caused by a careless camper. Cutting green trees is prohibited.

Knee or hip boots are desirable for landing the canoe and traversing boggy portages. More detailed maps and further information should be obtained from the Refuge Manager of the Kenai Moose Range. These maps are extremely helpful in locating the portages which are marked with small unobtrusive brown signs.

Canoes can be rented through: (1) Alaska Pioneer Canoers Assn., Box 931, Soldotna, Alaska 99669, phone 262-4003; (2) Pedersen's Moose River Resort, Mile 82, Star Route, Sterling (located at the junction of Moose River and the Sterling Highway), phone 262-4515; (3) Shaw Tool and Equipment Rental, Inc., Anchorage, phone 333-6561. The Canoers Assn. provides guided canoe trips.

This area is being considered for inclusion in the National Wilderness System.

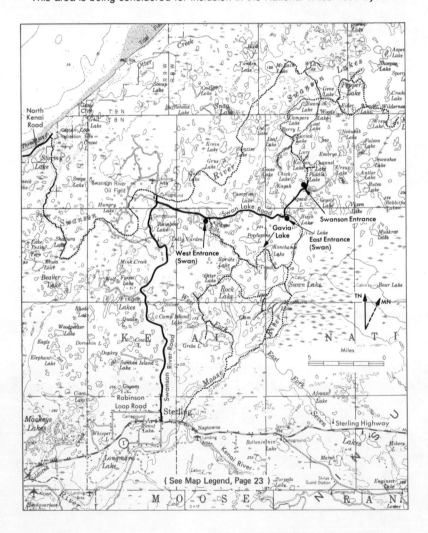

(See Map Legend, Page 23)

Common loon, Swan Lake canoe route (Photo by Callie Lustig)

KENAI PENINSULA

3 Seven Lakes Trail

Round trip 9 miles
Hiking time 4-6 hours
High point 450 feet
Elevation gain 100 feet
Best May—October
USGS maps Kenai B1, C1, C2
Kenai National Moose Range

A pleasant, easy walk for the whole family, largely through the Kenai burn of 1947, an area now growing up in young birch and spruce. It is especially enjoyable in early spring when birds are returning to the northland. The hiker may see the common loon, red-necked grebe, surf scoter, greater scaup, arctic tern, swan, pine grosbeak, spruce grouse, and numerous other birds. River otter even come out to play, so take a camera as well as a bird book. Occasional distant mountain vistas can be glimpsed across the various lakes.

At mile 57.8, Sterling Highway, turn south onto Skilak Loop road, and drive 9.2 miles to Engineer Lake Campground. Here Seven Lakes Trail (marked) begins, from the north end of the campground.

The trail first skirts the west side of Engineer Lake and climbs gently into the old burn (a reminder of man's carelessness). Two miles from Engineer Lake Campground, a junction is reached. Here a 0.7-mile side-trail goes to the west end of Hidden Lake. At Hidden Lake, the side-trail crosses a small stream in a stretch of unburned timber, and continues a short distance to a pleasant, undeveloped campsite on the shore of the lake.

From the junction with the side-trail to Hidden Lake, the main Seven Lakes Trail continues 1.5 miles north to Kelly Lake, skirting Hikers Lake on the way. The trail now follows the north shore of Kelly Lake to the developed camping area on the lake shore, then continues west from the camping area to Peterson Lake and the developed campsite there. Both Kelly Lake and Peterson Lake Campgrounds can be reached by road from mile 69 on the Sterling Highway, and the trail is well-marked at both camping areas. A car can be placed ahead of time at either of these campgrounds in order to avoid retracing steps. This may be especially worthwhile if small children are making the trip.

The trail continues northwest from Peterson Lake to cross the Sterling Highway at mile 70.2, but hiking beyond Peterson Lake is not recommended as that portion of the trail is boggy and not maintained.

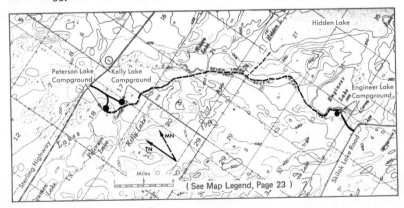

Engineer Lake, May (Photo by Nancy Simmerman)

The trail is easy walking over essentially flat terrain. Although good tent sites abound almost anywhere on the burn, and firewood is plentiful (fallen trees left from the '47 burn), water is generally not available except at the lakes.

Though not a spectacular hike by itself, this is an easy family trip, especially in conjunction with an overnight campout at one of the many campgrounds in the area. Fishing is good for rainbow trout and Dolly Varden in both Peterson and Kelly Lakes, and Hidden Lake is especially well-known for its lake trout as well as rainbows, Dolly Varden, and red salmon fry. The several road accesses to the trail at various points make shorter hikes possible for families with small children.

This should also make a pleasant winter ski or snowshoe tour. For winter use the best access is from the Sterling Highway, mile 69 entrance, to Kelly and Peterson Lakes. Skilak Loop road may not be plowed.

KENAI PENINSULA

4 Hidden Creek Trail/Kenai River Trail

Hidden Creek Trail
Round trip 3 miles
Hiking time 2-3 hours
High point 500 feet
Elevation gain 300 feet
Best May—October
USGS map Kenai B1
Kenai National Moose Range

Kenai River Trail
6 miles one way
Hiking time 4-6 hours
High point 550 feet
Elevation gain 350 feet
Winter: good anytime

An easy pleasant walk for the whole family down Hidden Creek Trail or Kenai River Trail to the mouth of Hidden Creek and to the shores of Skilak Lake. Either is a good winter trip on skis or snowshoes. Hikers may see spruce grouse, moose, coyote, wolf, and bear, and at the lake will find good fishing for rainbow trout, lake trout, Dolly Varden, silver salmon, and whitefish.

At mile 57.8 on the Sterling Highway turn south onto Skilak Loop road, a gravel road marked by a sign for Skilak Lake Recreation Area. After 4.5 miles look for a sign marking the beginning of **Hidden Creek Trail.** Park across the road from the trail marker.

The trail starts in the old Kenai burn of 1947, now well on its way to reforestation but still a grim reminder of what man's carelessness can do. Soon the hiker drops into wet meadows and coniferous forest with numerous streams crossing the trail. Logs have been laid across the trail to make walking drier, but sections are still wet. Continue through a pleasant forest of mixed coniferous and deciduous trees protecting a forest floor of moss, cranberry, crowberry, and Labrador tea. The trail ends on the shore of Skilak Lake where an endless supply of driftwood invites log-hopping and photographs.

A campground at the end of the trail provides refuse cans and outhouses. Nearby is a log shelter. A short walk to the east along the lake shore brings the hiker to Hidden Creek where it enters Skilak Lake. Pleasant mountain vistas across the lake.

Kenai River Trail, marked at the road, leaves Skilak Loop road 0.6 mile from its junction with the Sterling Highway, mile 57.8. Follow a dirt road leading 0.2 mile to the river and park. An unmarked trail parallels the river downstream for about 6 miles to a junction with Hidden Creek Trail.

(See Map Legend, Page 23)

Skilak Lake, May (Photo by Nancy Simmerman)

The intersection of the two trails may be difficult to find from the Hidden Creek Trail. In 1977, high water on the lake floated large quantities of driftwood over the intersection. At the intersection take the Kenai River Trail northeast which leads to and around a cabin on Hidden Creek. A short distance beyond the cabin, a trail branches to the left. This branch leads back to the main Hidden Creek Trail. To follow the Kenai River Trail north, take the right branch which leads to Hidden Creek below the bridge. Work upstream through a marshy area, and cross on a primitive log bridge. This area may be very wet in summer. On the other side of Hidden Creek the trail, not well marked, heads into the woods. Southbound, an arrow on a tree points to the bridge; cross and bear left to pick up the trail.

From the Kenai River Trail intersection, another trail heads southwest. This trail connects with Skilak Lake Lookout Trail (Trip 5) as shown on the map. This makes possible a nice circular trip as the entrances of the Hidden Creek Trail and the Skilak Lake Lookout Trail are only 0.7 mile apart on Skilak Loop road. It is more enjoyable if done starting from the Skilak Lake Lookout Trail due to the steepness of the connecting trail.

In winter Skilak Loop road may not be plowed. Check with the Refuge Manager in Kenai (phone: 283-4877) for current winter road conditions.

Skilak Lake from lookout point, May (Photo by Nancy Simmerman)

KENAI PENINSULA

5 Skilak Lake Lookout Trail

Round trip 5 miles
Hiking time 4-5 hours
High point 1400 feet
Elevation gain 700 feet
Best May—October
USGS map Kenai B1
Kenai National Moose Range

One of Alaska's few well-maintained and marked trails, through pleasant woods, with a lovely view at the end. Good for children who can walk this far. Spruce grouse, moose, and bear may be seen. Water is plentiful along the trail except near the end.

At mile 57.8 on the Sterling Highway turn south onto Skilak Loop road, a gravel road marked by a sign for Skilak Lake Recreation Area. Drive 5.4 miles on this road to a sign marking the Skilak Lake Lookout Trail.

The trail leaves the road to the south and climbs gently through woods. Springs and streamlets cross the trail at more or less regular intervals. Occasional glimpses of Skilak Lake appear. Near the end the trail climbs more steeply to a knob from which there is a panoramic view of Skilak Lake and the surrounding mountains to the south, Kenai Mountains to the northeast, and Mt. Spurr and Mt. Gerdine to the northwest. The view is well worth the trip.

There are no developed campsites on the trail but there are six public campgrounds located along the Skilak Loop road. This is a good trail for skis or snowshoes in winter.

The Kenai River Trail (see Hidden Creek Trail, Trip 4) connects with the Skilak Lake Lookout Trail as shown on the map.

Starting with the Skilak Lake Lookout Trail, three circular trips are possible in combination with the Hidden Creek Trail and the two entrances of the Kenai River Trail (see map). It is more enjoyable to start from the Skilak Lake Lookout Trail because of the steepness of the connecting trail.

In winter Skilak Loop road may not be plowed. Check with the Refuge Manager in Kenai (phone: 283-4877) for current winter road conditions.

39

KENAI PENINSULA

6 Fuller Lakes

Round trip 5½ miles
Hiking time 3-5 hours
High point 1690 feet
Elevation gain 1400 feet
Best June—October
USGS maps Kenai B1, C1
Kenai National Moose Range

A jewel of a lake situated just at timberline, surrounded by scattered hemlocks, spruce, and grassy meadows alternating with scrub willow. Another smaller lake just below timberline. Tempting camping and a good family trip, though some uphill hiking is involved. When there is enough snow this is a good winter cross-country ski or snowshoe trip for those able to handle moderately steep grades.

Hikers can make Upper Fuller Lake their destination (5½ miles round trip, elevation gain 1400 feet) but some will want to climb the ridge to the west (high point 3520 feet). The hardiest will want to follow the ridge and descend by an alternate trail to Sterling Highway mile 61 (11½ miles, total elevation gain about 5000 feet, including ups and downs).

To reach Upper Fuller Lake drive to about mile 57.1 on the Sterling Highway. Park there at a pull-off on the south side of the road (300 feet elevation).

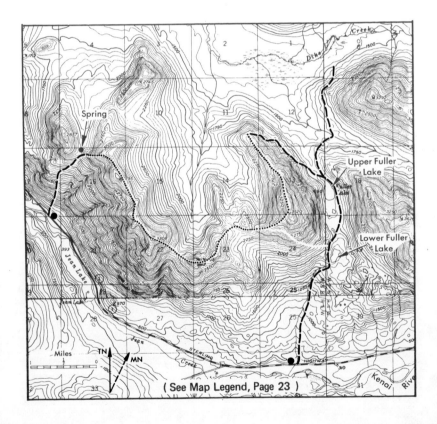

(See Map Legend, Page 23)

40

Lower Fuller Lake, October (Photo by Nancy Simmerman)

An old road blocked by logs and marked by a sign for Fuller Lakes Trail leads north. Follow this road which soon becomes a well-defined trail and climbs through forest and meadows, and occasionally along a tiny stream. Look back frequently for views of Skilak Lake and the mountains to the southeast. After about a mile the trail forks; take the right-hand fork along the stream. At Lower Fuller Lake cross the stream on a beaver dam and continue to follow the main path along the left side of the lake and on to Upper Fuller Lake, an ideal overnight spot. Arrows have been put up marking the trail, but bears sometimes twist them or tear them down. Lower Fuller Lake is popular with grayling fishermen; Dolly Varden are found in Upper Fuller Lake.

Ridges and knobs beckon from the lake, and brush presents little obstacle to exploration. The trail continues around the east side of Upper Fuller Lake and then branches. The right branch stops short of Dike Creek. The left branch leads up onto the ridge. This trail crosses the outlet of the lake almost immediately after the lake. The trail here may be overgrown, but cross the outlet anyway and pick up the trail to the left of the small knob on the other side.

To go over the ridge is a long strenuous 1-day trip. A high meadow and spring at the western end of the ridge offer a possible campsite (see map for approximate location). Above brushline the route is unmarked. The only water on the ridge is the spring or occasional snowbanks. The ridge trail was not checked by the authors.

The ridge route terminates just east of milepost 61, Sterling Highway. Park at the gravel pit on the south side of the highway. This end of the trail is not marked. Taken from this end the trail climbs **very** steeply and footing is slippery on mossy and grassy slopes.

This area is being considered for inclusion in the National Wilderness System.

Kenai Lake to Skilak Lake: one-way trip 23 miles
Allow 1 day
Gradient 14 feet per mile
Best May—October
USGS maps Seward B8, Kenai B1

7 Kenai River Canoe Trip

Skilak Lake to Kenai: 51 miles
1 or 2 days
Gradient 4 feet per mile
Best May—October
USGS maps Kenai B2, B3, C2, C3, C4
Kenai National Moose Range

A good trip for the intermediate or experienced canoeist or kayaker, though not for the beginner because of swift cold water and rapids. For experienced boatmen there is just enough white water to make the trip interesting. The scenery ranges from the mountains of Kenai Lake to the coastal flats surrounding Kenai village. Good fishing and many different water birds. Gulls and cormorants nest on rocks in Skilak Lake 2-3 miles south of the Kenai River inlet.

Eight entrances or exits for this trip make many variations possible. A good one-day trip, relatively easy for the intermediate except in high water, is from Cooper Landing (1) to mile 57½, Sterling Highway (4). This has one set of Class III rapids at Schooner Bend. Keep against the right bank. For rafters and experienced kayakers, a longer one-day trip is from Cooper Landing (1) to Hidden Creek (7). This has 2 miles of Class IV rapids in the Kenai canyon; experience and a splash cover are necessary. Boats can be paddled or lined up lazy Hidden Creek to the road, a distance of about 2 miles. Be prepared to portage around the fish weir.

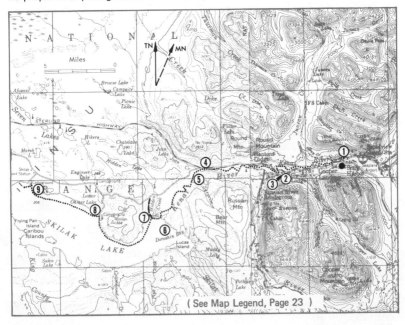

(See Map Legend, Page 23)

Kenai River below Kenai Lake, May (Photo by Nancy Simmerman)

Skilak Lake (9) to Kenai (15) is considered Class II (medium) canoeing except for its single stretch of Class III at Naptowne rapids. Boats may be portaged or lined around all rapids except those in Kenai River canyon. Skilak Lake itself is subject to high winds and can therefore be dangerous. Stay close to shore.

Major points of interest along the way are: (1) entrance, Cooper Landing at Kenai River bridge, mile 47.7, Sterling Highway; 23 miles to Upper Skilak Lake Campground, 81 miles to Kenai; (2) entrance, bridge, mile 53 Sterling Highway; (3) Schooner Bend rapids immediately after bridge, Class III; (4) exit-entrance, roadside

Kenai River canyon, May (Photo by Nancy Simmerman)

pull-off by Kenai River, about mile 57½, Sterling Highway; (5) Kenai River canyon, 2 miles of Class IV rapids; (6) Skilak Lake, about 3 miles below canyon, stay close to shore; (7) Hidden Creek and Trail (Trip 4) to Skilak Loop road, 30 minutes away by foot; (8) Upper Skilak Lake Campground, 6 miles down lake; 10 miles on Skilak Loop road from mile 57.8, Sterling Highway; (9) entrance, Lower Skilak Lake Campground, 7 miles from upper campground, 16 miles from Sterling Highway mile 57.8; 51 miles to Kenai; (10) Skilak Lake outlet, Kenai River, 2 miles from lower campground; (11) Class III rapids, 10 miles down river; (12) confluence of Moose and Kenai Rivers shortly after rapids, entrance-exit, Moose River bridge, Sterling Highway about mile 84, less than ⅛ mile up lazy Moose River; (13) entrance-exit, Kenai River bridge at Soldotna, mile 95.9 Sterling Highway; (14) tidal action influences river flow beginning halfway between Soldotna and Kenai; (15) exit, Kenai, at city dock.

Safety dictates that boaters inspect white water before trying it. The Schooner Bend rapids can be seen from the side-road to the Chugach National Forest Russian River Campground, at mile 52.7, Sterling Highway. To inspect Kenai River canyon rapids, drive to Sterling Highway mile 57.8 and turn south on Skilak Loop road for 2.2 miles to a sign for the Kenai River Trail. Park and follow the trail about ½ mile to its intersection with the Kenai River Trail (Trip 4). Cross the Kenai River Trail and continue straight ahead toward the river, bushwhacking to the canyon rim. The Kenai River Trail does not closely follow the river at this point. The difficulty of any of these rapids will vary according to water level.

Boaters should wear lifejackets, and two or more boats should travel together, though a safe distance apart. Wear enough clothing or wet suits to protect against the cold water in case of capsizing. The extreme cold of the water can cause rapid exhaustion and even loss of consciousness. Much of the trip is not near a road and help is far away.

Classifications of river difficulty used here were taken from the Bureau of Land Management (BLM) ratings. The "difficulty" ratings used range from I to VI. Some whitewater paddlers feel that BLM has in some cases overrated the difficulty of Alaska rivers. Nevertheless, the Kenai River canyon rapids are not suitable for inexperienced paddlers in open canoes.

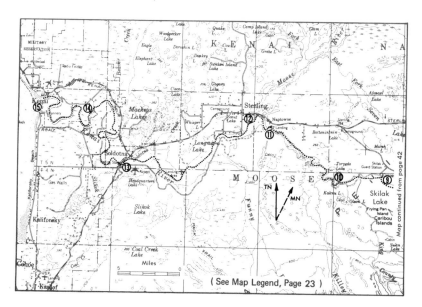

Map continued from page 42

(See Map Legend, Page 23)

KENAI PENINSULA

8 Russian Lakes — Cooper Lake Trail

Lower Russian Lake round trip 6 miles
Hiking time 3 hours
High point 550 feet
Elevation gain 200 feet
Best May—October
USGS map Seward B8

Upper Russian Lake round trip 24 miles
Allow 2 days
High point 690 feet
Elevation gain 340 feet
Best May—October
USGS maps Seward B8, Kenai B1

Cooper Lake 21 miles one way
Allow 2 days
High point 1450 feet
Elevation gain 150 feet
Best June—October
USGS maps Seward B8, Kenai B1
Chugach National Forest

A well-traveled trail to scenic Lower Russian Lake or beyond to Upper Russian Lake. Or take the entire route from Cooper Lake to Upper Russian Lake and out the Russian Lakes trail. A beautiful forest walk with crystal-clear streams cascading into Russian River, brilliant wildflowers, moose, bear, and berries in season. Excellent fishing. Views of glaciered mountains across Upper Russian Lake.

To hike to either of the Russian Lakes drive to about mile 52.7, Sterling Highway. Turn south here onto a side-road marked "Chugach National Forest Campground, Russian River." (Do not confuse with National Moose Range Kenai-Russian River Campground located near mile 55 and Sportsman's Lodge.) Follow the side-road 0.8 mile to a sign and parking area for Russian Lakes trail. Park here.

The trail to both Russian Lakes begins at this point (elevation 350 feet). The trip to Lower Russian Lake (elevation 550 feet) is a nice 1-day family trip over a good trail, a pretty woodland walk high above Russian River and partly through the 1969 burn. In fishing season the area is crowded with fishermen. Occasional fishermen's trails branch off the main trail but the main trail is marked. Shortly before Lower Russian Lake the trail crosses "Rendezvous Creek" on a bridge. To reach Lower Russian Lake take a right-hand fork in the trail just before the bridge. This fork parallels

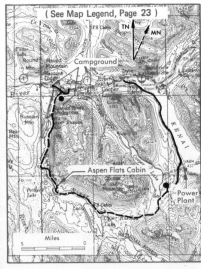

Poppies, July (Photo by Nancy Simmerman)

Float planes on Upper Russian Lake, July (Photo by Nancy Simmerman)

"Rendezvous Creek" to its confluence with Russian River. Five tent sites with fire rings have been provided along this trail. From Russian River follow the fishermen's trail upstream about ¼ mile to the lake or downstream about ¼ mile to Russian River cascades. The fishermen's trail can also be followed downstream to Russian River Campground.

The second hiking possibility, to Upper Russian Lake (elevation 690 feet), is more demanding because it is longer. Follow the main trail across "Rendezvous Creek," above Lower Russian Lake, and on to the south for about 8½ miles. The main trail is marked so forks should not be confusing. The Chugach National Forest maintains 2 cabins, one at Aspen Flats, 9 miles from the Kenai River trailhead, and one at Upper Russian Lake, 13 miles. Make reservations with the Forest Service in Seward or Anchorage.

A third possibility is to hike from Cooper Lake to Russian River Campground. Leave a car at the campground and drive to Snug Harbor Road at mile 47.8, Sterling Highway. Follow this road southeast to a marked parking area about 11 miles from the Sterling Highway. Starting at the Cooper Lake end of this trail is recommended because it is the higher end of the trail (about 1300 feet). The nine-mile trail to Upper Russian Lake is a pleasant meander through attractive taiga dotted with pothole lakes.

The trail to Lower and Upper Russian Lakes makes a good winter ski or snowshoe trip, (See "Avalanches," page 17.) but it is also used by snowmobilers. The Russian River Campground road is not plowed in winter. The Snug Harbor Road is kept open to Cooper Lake Power Plant on Kenai Lake. If taking the Cooper Lake to Russian Lake trail on skis, starting at the Cooper Lake end is much pleasanter.

The trail is closed to use by motorized vehicles from April 1 through November 30 and closed to horses from April 1 through June 30.

9 Crescent Lake — Carter Lake

Via Crescent Creek round trip 12.4 miles
Hiking time 5-8 hours
High point 1454 feet
Elevation gain 864 feet
Best June—October
USGS maps Seward B7, B8, C7, C8

Via Carter Lake round trip 8 miles
Hiking time 3-5 hours
High point 1454 feet
Elevation gain 954 feet
Good all year
USGS maps Seward B7, C7
Chugach National Forest

A lovely walk over an excellent trail to a pretty lake almost at timberline. A glorious September hike through the golds and reds of autumn. Good for families with small children (who can walk that far) if reservations are made for overnight use of the Chugach National Forest cabin located at the west end of Crescent Lake. A rowboat goes with the cabin, and fishing for grayling is good. The opposite (east) end of Crescent Lake can be reached via a shorter but steeper trail that goes first to Carter Lake. There are few fish at this end of Crescent Lake, and none in Carter Lake. Six miles of steep brushy slope separate the ends of Crescent Lake. Unless fish or the cabin are the main objectives, the east end of the lake is a nice alternate trip.

At mile 45 on the Sterling Highway (at Sunrise Inn—about 7 miles west of the junction of the Sterling and Seward Highways) turn south on a road marked "Quartz Creek Recreation Area." The road forks in about a mile. Take the left fork. Drive 2.1 miles to a sign for the Crescent Creek Trail.

The Crescent Creek trail, a broad pathway, starts directly across the road from the parking area at an elevation of 600 feet. The trail winds gently upward through birch-aspen woods along a tiny stream, climbs over a low ridge, and drops into Crescent Creek canyon. Follow Crescent Creek upstream to open country, cross the

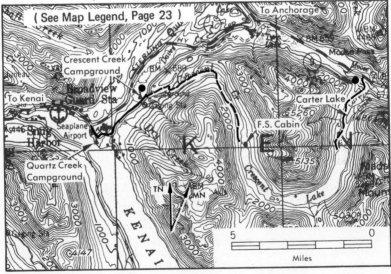

(See Map Legend, Page 23)

Crescent Lake, west end, September (Photo by Nancy Simmerman)

creek on a bridge, and continue, often well above the creek. The trail now wanders through patches of woods and through avalanche-cleared swatches, finally emerging in a broad open meadow dotted with trees. Cross Crescent Creek again on bridge near the lake outlet. The cabin is a short distance along the lake shore beyond the bridge crossing (lake elevation 1454 feet). Make reservations through the Chugach National Forest in Anchorage or Seward. Easy access to high country from this area.

To reach Crescent Lake via Carter Lake drive the Seward Highway to mile 33.1. The trail leaves from a parking area here on the west side of the highway (elevation 500 feet). (This is an old jeep trail originally built by the city of Seward as part of a now-discarded plan for a water resource. It is now another sad example of what uncontrolled use of motorized vehicles can do to soft terrain. Hopefully, the scar will heal in time.)

On foot head up the jeep road which is steep in places. After reaching Carter Lake, at about 2 miles, elevation 1486 feet, a foot trail continues around the west side of the lake and on to Crescent Lake. In winter this trail makes an excellent ski tour; skiers can continue across Crescent Lake to the cabin.

There are good campsites at both ends of the lake. Water is available, but the wood supply is primarily brush. Moose and bear may be spotted in summer, wolverine occasionally in winter.

Both trails are closed to motorized vehicles from April 1 through November 30 and to horses from April 1 through June 30. Crescent Creek trail is hazardous in winter due to avalanches. (See "Avalanches," page 17.)

KENAI PENINSULA

KENAI PENINSULA

10 Race Point

Round trip 3 miles
Hiking time 44½ minutes to 6 hours
High point 3022 feet
Elevation gain 2900 feet
Best April—October
USGS map Seward A7

In 1915, the year the railroad from Seward founded Anchorage, a bet in Seward started a race still repeated every 4th of July. The runners in this mountain marathon start from the town center, near sea level, climb to Race Point, 3022 feet, at the end of the southeast ridge of Mt. Marathon, and return. The record is 44 minutes, 11 seconds, set in 1974 by Bill Spencer. Independence Day is the most exciting time to

Seward Harbor and Resurrection Bay from Race Point trail, September (Photo by Nancy Simmerman)

make the climb, whether in the race or not, but it is a good hike anytime during the summer.

There are two trails to Race Point. The Hikers' Trail is extraordinarily steep, but the Runners' Trail is even steeper. Fortunately, the Hikers' Trail provides a spectacular view of Seward and Resurrection Bay, giving ready excuse for pause. The hiker may choose to go up the Hikers' Trail and down the Runners'; the two are within walking distance at their lower ends.

To reach the Hikers' Trail find First Avenue in Seward, the street which runs along the base of Mt. Marathon. Drive to its intersection with Monroe Street, 2 blocks north of the hospital. Park here.

Across from Monroe Street is a dirt road marked "Marathon Municipal Water Supply." Walk up this road to its end at a building and beautiful waterfall. From here follow a foot trail steeply uphill through a forest of large and lovely hemlock. Abruptly the forest ends on a shelf, and alders take over. Brush crowds the trail in spots, but this is still the most pleasant way up.

The Runners' Trail is better known and marked by signs — but steeper. At the intersection of Jefferson Street and First Avenue (by the Seward Hospital) there is a sign for the Mt. Marathon Trail. Drive west on Jefferson Street into Lowell Creek Canyon. The trail begins in a small gravel pit just beyond the water storage tanks. The first section of the trail is steepest, requiring use of hands in spots. The runners ascend the ridge to the right of the gully and return in the scree of the gully.

On a ridge at the head of the gully the two Runners' routes join the Hikers' Trail right at brushline, at about 1700 feet. The Hikers' Trail here is hard to find on the way down; note this spot carefully if you will be returning on that trail. From the junction follow the ridge upward. Keep left on the ridge for better footing; the wider right-hand track is better for descent. The trail becomes poorly defined on the rocky ridge, but by switchbacking up the slope one gains the broad "summit" at 3022 feet. Unless you are a runner, sit awhile to enjoy the vast view of Resurrection Bay and the glacier-streaked mountains across it. Look for ptarmigan, parka squirrels, marmots, mountain goats, and Dall sheep.

There are often snow patches near the top well into July, but these can be avoided. The lower part of the trail is open early in spring and still provides glorious views. The gully, used by the runners for descent, has snow late in the year and cliffs always. Fun for the adventurous. The true summit of Mt. Marathon (4750 feet) requires experience and mountaineering gear.

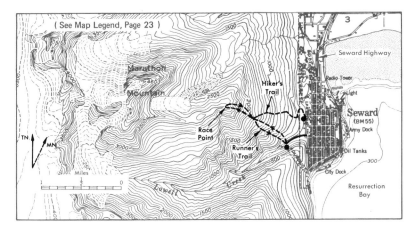

KENAI PENINSULA

11 Lost Lake

Round trip 14 miles; traverse 15 miles
Hiking time 7-10 hours
High point 1920 feet
Elevation gain 1800 feet; via Primrose 1500 feet
Best late June—September
USGS maps Seward A7, B7
Chugach National Forest

In July this is perhaps the most beautiful and photogenic trail the Kenai Peninsula has to offer. The trail passes through hemlock and spruce woods and emerges above treeline to tundra and flowered meadows accented by stands of weathered hemlock. The area was at one time heavily glaciered. Now brilliant blue lakes fill every depression, reflecting the snow-covered mountains of the surrounding country. At the end of the trail is Lost Lake, of azure-blue water, forced into a strange shape by the topography. The area invites the hiker to camp overnight, and explore the surrounding alpine country. Water is plentiful but firewood scarce, so take a cook stove. A few small fish (rainbow) populate Lost Lake, and marmots abound in the nearby rock slides. This is a good family trail and a good winter snowshoe or cross-country ski trip.

Drive to milepost 5.0 on the Seward Highway where there is a National Forest sign for Lost Lake on the west side of the highway. Turn here into a parking area and leave your car. The elevation at this point is just over 100 feet.

On foot follow a marked logging road west until it becomes a well-defined Forest Service trail. At 0.9 mile up the trail a snowmachine trail branches off to the right (marked by a sign picturing a snowmobile). Follow the left-hand trail which winds through heavily timbered canyons and is very pleasant. Occasionally Resurrection Bay can be seen glistening in the distance. The latter part of the route is entirely above brushline. About mile 6 the trail emerges on a glacier-scarred bedrock bench. Another mile brings the hiker to Lost Lake, at 1920 feet elevation.

In August salmonberries can be found along the trail near mile 4. In some years snow may persist on the trail into July, making the portion above timberline hard to follow.

Attaining the summit of Mt. Ascension (5710 feet) is a goal best left to mountaineers who may find use for ice axe and crampons. Climbing partway up the steep slopes to a lower viewpoint, however, is certainly possible. A walk around the south side of the lake and up the valley from the west end (easy walking over firm alpine tundra) will bring the hiker a splendid view of the steep north side of Mt. Ascension and the increased possibility of seeing black bear or goats on the mountainside.

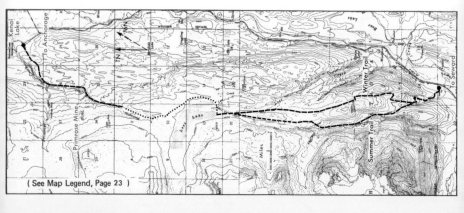

(See Map Legend, Page 23)

Hikers on Lost Lake trail, July (Photo by Nancy Simmerman)

A 15-mile traverse between Lost Lake and Kenai Lake is possible. To walk from Lost Lake to Kenai Lake, wade icy, knee-deep Lost Creek at the lake outlet, and continue around the lake to a low pass on the north side. Beyond the pass pick up the trail as it parallels Porcupine Creek on a ridge on its east side. Do not follow the orange markers leading into the forest before the pass — this is a winter snowmobile trail.

To find the Kenai Lake trailhead, turn off the Seward Highway at mile 17.1 at a sign for Primrose Campground. The trailhead is in the campground parking lot and should be marked by a sign.

The trail, from mile 4 to the end at Kenai Lake, is closed to all motorized vehicles, including snowmobiles, from April 1 through November 30, and closed to horses from April 1 through June 30.

KENAI PENINSULA

12 Ptarmigan Lake

Round trip 6 or 7 miles
Hiking time 4-5 hours
High point 900 feet
Elevation gain 450 feet
Best May—October
USGS maps Seward B7, B6
Chugach National Forest

A turquoise beauty reflecting the mountains that surround it. Magnificent views from the trail. A good overnight for children. Two trails lead from the highway to the lake, and a 4-mile (one way) extension of the trail continues around the lake to the east end. The upper trail (about 3 miles) is shorter and easier; the lower trail (3.4 miles) follows the creek over considerably more hilly and difficult terrain. Fishermen will find grayling, salmon, Dolly Varden, and rainbow trout in Ptarmigan Creek, and grayling in Ptarmigan Lake. Avalanche hazard precludes winter use of either trail. (See "Avalanches," page 17.)

To find the **upper trail** drive to mile 24.2 on the Seward Highway. Here a gravel road turns east across the railroad tracks. This road is opposite and slightly north of Chugach National Forest Trail River Campground. Cross the tracks and park by the tracks (elevation about 450 feet).

On foot continue east on the road leading to a cabin and frame house. Respect the private property along the road and do not litter. The Ptarmigan Lake trail begins as a rough jeep road near the log cabin. A Forest Service sign marked the beginning but the trail is not maintained so signs may be down. After about a mile there is a clearing, the remains of a burned cabin, and a creek crossing. Just beyond this the Ptarmigan Lake trail leaves the road to the right; this junction may be marked with a Forest Service sign. Leaving the road, the trail climbs a low timbered ridge, then contours along the mountainside at 900 feet elevation, well above the valley floor. Look for glimpses of Ptarmigan and Kenai Lakes. Shortly, the lower trail intersects this trail. Continue straight ahead and soon Ptarmigan Lake is reached, at 753 feet elevation.

This can be the destination for a picnic or overnight camping. (There is abundant driftwood on the beach.) Or continue around the north shore of the lake about 4 miles to the eastern end which also offers good campsites. Neither end is at present developed. Fallen trees and an eroded bank or two must be circumnavigated before reaching the far end of the lake, but the trip is worthwhile.

The **lower trail** leaves from the picnic area of the Chugach National Forest

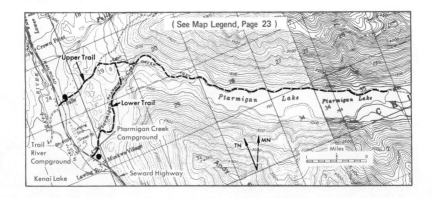

(See Map Legend, Page 23)

Ptarmigan Lake, June (Photo by Nancy Simmerman)

Ptarmigan Creek Campground at mile 23.2 on the Seward Highway. From the picnic area the trail follows the creek upstream, but occasionally turns from the stream to wander through a quiet rock grotto or over a scenic knob. The mileage for the lake (2.5) given on the Ptarmigan Creek National Forest sign at the campground is incorrect. It is 3.4 miles. When a large open meadow is reached at 2.2 miles the creek trail appears to continue straight ahead. Another trail branches off to the left and can be seen climbing the hillside. Follow this steep left fork up the hillside to its intersection with the high trail, then take a right turn to Ptarmigan Lake.

Ideally, the hiker could enter on one of the trails and exit via the other. In this case, add 1 mile for the highway distance between starting points of each trail. Owners of airplanes can land on the Lawing airstrip near the beginning of the upper trail. From the strip follow the railroad tracks north to the first gravel road crossing the tracks; turn right on this and continue to the National Forest trail marker.

Originally, Ptarmigan Lake trail continued into Paradise Valley and then paralleled Snow River back to the railroad. This trail, now badly overgrown, was built by the Civilian Conservation Corps in the 1930s.

The trail is closed to use by motorized vehicles from April 1 through November 30 and closed to horses from April 1 through June 30.

55

KENAI PENINSULA

13 Johnson Pass

Traverse 21 miles
Allow 2 days
High point 1500 feet
Elevation gain 1000 feet
Best June-September
USGS maps Seward C6, C7
Chugach National Forest

In the early 1900s the first road was built on the Kenai Peninsula, a wagon trail from Seward to Hope over Johnson Pass. It was part of the old Seward mail trail, and was maintained by the military. The hiking trail now follows portions of that route; traces of the old trail and of abandoned cabins and wagons can still be found.

The Forest Service has done a vast amount of work "improving" and re-routing the trail to its own specifications for hiking. Bridges now cross all streams, and the trail is broad and deep.

Drive to mile 63.8 Seward Highway, just south of Granite Creek Guard Station (96 miles south of Anchorage). A marked side-road leads to the Granite Creek (northern) trailhead and parking area. The southern trailhead, marked, is at mile 32.5, Seward Highway, near Upper Trail Lake. The trip is equally pleasant taken from either direction.

From the Granite Creek trailhead, the route winds through open meadows and forest. At the Bench Creek bridge (mile 3.8) the trail enters the V-shaped Bench Creek valley, and follows the creek to its source at Bench Lake and Ohio Creek (mile 8.9). Pleasant short trips to Center Creek (mile 2.2) and Bench Creek are possible, as well as a hike to the pass and return (20 miles round trip), or the entire 23-mile traverse.

After crossing Ohio Creek the trail follows the eastern shore of Bench Lake and climbs imperceptibly to Johnson Pass, mile 10 (elevation 1500 feet). South of Johnson Lake, the trail parallels Johnson Creek, but is above it in the woods. At about mile 19 the trail emerges on the shore of Upper Trail Lake. It follows the shore to the southern trailhead at mile 32.5 Seward Highway.

Good campsites can be found at the south end of Johnson Lake (mile 11), where wood is available, and at Johnson Pass (mile 10), which is above timberline. Fish inhabit both lakes.

The southern portion of the trail, from Upper Trail Lake to Johnson Lake, makes a good winter ski tour except in periods of extreme avalanche hazard. (See "Av-

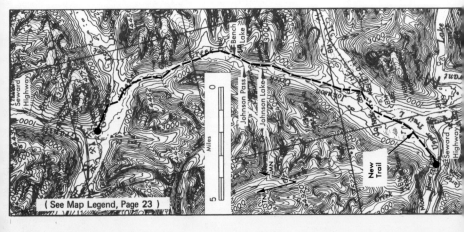

(See Map Legend, Page 23)

Johnson Lake, July (Photo by Nancy Simmerman)

alanches," page 17.) The northern end of the trail, from the Granite Creek trailhead to the Bench Creek crossing at mile 3.8, is also a good ski trip and is open only to non-motorized uses. Between mile 3.8 and Johnson Pass there is avalanche hazard. The public use cabin at Johnson Pass was destroyed by an avalanche in the winter of 1974-75.

The trail is closed to motorized vehicles from April 1 through November 30 and to horses from April 1 through June 30. The northern end of the trail, to mile 3.8, is closed to snowmobiles.

KENAI PENINSULA

14 Resurrection Pass Trail System

One-way trip 38 miles
Allow 3 to 7 days
High point 2600 feet
Elevation gain 2200 feet
Best June—September
USGS maps Seward B8, C7, C8, D8
Chugach National Forest

Hikers wanting a long backpack on a good trail, with cabins and fishing at intervals, through the always beautiful Alaskan mountains, will find the Resurrection Pass trail system on the Kenai Peninsula the answer. The standard route, between Hope and Schooner Bend, 38 miles, can be done in 3 days by sturdy hikers and 5 or more days by families. Time spent shuttling a car about 50 miles to the opposite end of the trail is in addition to estimated hiking time. (This route, from Kenai Lake to Hope, was one of the trails traveled in the late 1890s by gold seekers coming from Resurrection Bay to the Turnagain gold fields near Hope.) Alternate trips are: (1) Hope to the Seward Highway via Devil's Creek or Summit Creek (31 miles); (2) Devil's Creek to Schooner Bend (27 miles — 2 days); (3) in Summit Creek and out Devil's Creek (19½ miles — 1

Dall sheep, ewe, September (Photo by Nancy Simmerman)

day for strong, fast hikers). All trails except Summit Creek (an old miner's trail in good condition) are maintained (with bridges) by the U.S. Forest Service.

To hike from Hope to Schooner Bend drive to mile 56.3 on the Seward Highway (68 miles south of Anchorage). Turn north here and drive most of the 17 miles to Hope. Just before Hope turn left on Palmer Creek Road; in 0.6 mile turn right on Resurrection Creek Road; and drive about 3½ miles to a sign marking the trail beginning at 500 feet elevation. The cabins are well spaced for a 5-day trip, although families may choose a 7-day trip utilizing more cabins. Faster hikers may prefer to take tents. (Make reservations well ahead with the Chugach National Forest office.)

The trail follows wooded Resurrection Creek valley to the creek headwaters in the open tundra of Resurrection Pass, then down Juneau Creek through forest and by lovely lakes, to the Sterling Highway. Points of interest: (1) Caribou Creek cabin, mile 7.1; (2) Fox Creek campsite, mile 11.6; (3) East Creek cabin, mile 14.4; (4) Resurrection Pass, 2600 feet, mile 19.3; (5) Summit Creek trail, about mile 20; (6) Devil's Pass cabin and Devil's Pass trail, mile 21.4; (7) Swan Lake cabin, and access to West Swan Lake cabin, boat for cabin renters, fishing, mile 25.8; (8) Juneau Lake cabin, boat, fishing, mile 29.1; (9) Romig cabin on Juneau Lake, boat, fishing, mile 30; (10) ½-mile side-trail to Trout Lake cabin, boat, fishing, mile 31.8; (11) Juneau Creek Falls, mile 34.1. The 38.6-mile-long trail terminates near mile 53.1, Sterling Highway just west of the Kenai River bridge.

The Devil's Creek trail begins at mile 39.4 on the Seward Highway at 1000 feet elevation. The trail and parking lot are marked by a Chugach National Forest trailhead sign on the highway.

The Summit Creek trail leaves the Seward Highway at mile 43.8. Park in a pull-out on the east side of the Seward Highway, just north of mile 43.9, or drive a short distance up a rutted side-road to the powerline and park. The remainder of the dirt road continues to erode and is impassable to standard vehicles. On foot, follow the old road along Summit Creek until it becomes a foot path. This trail begins at 1700 feet, climbs over two passes (3450 and 3350 feet), and descends to Resurrection Pass.

Watch for Kenai brown bear during fall and winter. Sheep, moose, marmots, and many wildflowers inhabit various parts of the route. No firewood is available in the pass. This is a good winter trip on skis or snowshoes, but winter blizzards in the pass are possible. Devil's Creek and Summit Creek trails are subject to avalanches in winter. (See "Avalanches," page 17.) The entire Resurrection Pass trail system is closed to use by motorized vehicles, including snowmobiles, from February 15 through November 30 and closed to horses from April 1 through June 30.

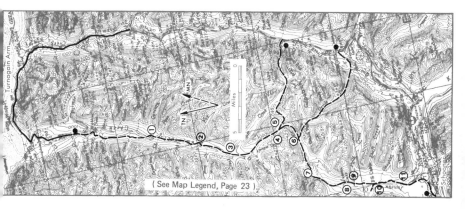

(See Map Legend, Page 23)

KENAI PENINSULA

15 Palmer Creek

Round trip 2 miles
Hiking time 1-2 hours
High point 2950 feet
Elevation gain 750 feet
Best July—September
USGS map Seward D7
Chugach National Forest

A lovely tundra-covered valley punctuated by random weathered hemlock. A high, hanging valley cradling two alpine lakes. A tumbling waterfall, a wildflower paradise. Good for children and grandparents alike. High above the old mining community of Hope. The only sobering note is the last 5 miles of the road — high, narrow, winding — driveable, however, by most two-wheel-drive cars with sufficiently high clearance. Unsafe for campers and trailers.

Gold was first discovered on Palmer Creek by George Palmer in 1894. A rush to the Turnagain area gold fields took place in 1896. Two towns, Hope and Sunrise, grew out of it, and as many as 5000 people were reported living here in 1898. Palmer Creek was the site of early placer mining and later lode mining, beginning in 1911 with John Hirshey's Lucky Strike vein, and continuing into the 1930s.

At mile 56.3 on the Seward Highway (68 miles south of Anchorage) turn north onto the 17-mile gravel side-road leading to Hope. Shortly before Hope turn left on Palmer Creek Road. In 0.6 mile, at the next major intersection, continue straight, still on Palmer Creek Road. Follow this road about 7 miles to the Chugach National Forest Coeur d' Alene Campground (suitable for tent camping only). The road is not maintained beyond here; continue up it about 5 miles farther to its end at the abandoned Swetmann Camp. Park near the old mine buildings.

A steep footpath climbs the hillside to the east and leads to the hanging valley with the alpine lakes. The trail begins near the cabins and just before (north of) the streams, at about 2200 feet elevation. Although steep, it is short (less than a mile) — fine for children and for agile older people. On the way the trail passes a pretty waterfall. A larger and lower waterfall can be reached by cutting across the hillside to the right (south) below the steepest part of the trail. This makes a nice detour on the way back down. The lakes, nestled below sheer rock walls at 2950 feet, make a good picnic spot; a few small fish are reported.

Families may also enjoy a stroll upvalley from their parked cars to a small knob about a mile away. A tiny gemlike tarn lies hidden behind it. Nice valley views from the

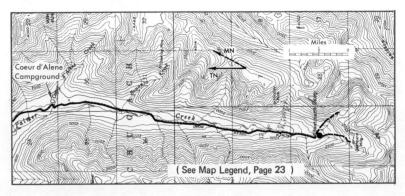

(See Map Legend, Page 23)

Unnamed lake above Palmer Creek, August (Photo by Nancy Simmerman)

knob. Hikers who enjoy rock scrambling will find inviting ridges and small peaks in the area. A particularly easy ridge to climb onto is the one to the southwest of the two high lakes, separating them from the main valley. From the lakes one can easily reach the 4000-foot level on this ridge and enjoy even better views.

There is plenty of water en route to the lakes but none on the higher ridges. Camping near the road's end or at the lakes is possible (no firewood) but heavy human use of the area would be destructive to the tundra. Good campsites (and firewood) are available at the Coeur d'Alene Campground.

Fun fishing for children in the beaver ponds along Palmer Creek, which has golden fin trout. The mine buildings are private property and should be left alone. Because of snow, northern exposure, and a narrow valley the road cannot usually be driven until July. Even in July and August snow and ice patches may remain along the stream and at the lakes.

Considerable avalanche danger makes this area hazardous for winter use. (See "Avalanches," page 17.)

61

KENAI PENINSULA

16 Hope Point

Round trip 5 miles
Hiking time 4½-8 hours
High point 3708 feet
Elevation gain 3630 feet
Best May—October
USGS map Seward D8
Chugach National Forest

A lovely though very steep hike near Hope, offering spectacular views of Turnagain Arm from a different angle than is usually available. Most hiking near Turnagain Arm starts from the Anchorage side. From Hope Point, in contrast, the hiker can look north across the Arm and put in perspective those familiar Chugach Mountains southeast of Anchorage. Take extra maps to help locate favorite spots: Seward D7, Anchorage A7, A8.

At mile 56.3 on the Seward Highway (68 miles south of Anchorage) turn north onto the 17-mile gravel side-road leading to Hope. Go around Hope, continue another mile to the road's end at the Chugach National Forest Porcupine Creek Campground, and park near the campground entrance, elevation about 80 feet.

Follow the campground road across nearby tiny Porcupine Creek. An unmarked foot trail follows the right-hand (north) side of the stream, leading the hiker on a lovely creekside walk beside water tumbling gently over mossy rocks. The first ⅓ mile is a gentle meander along the stream under a canopy of large alder. The trail then climbs the bluff to the right and continues steeply upward through forest. Soon the trees thin to a meadow parkland studded with evergreens. Climb far enough to get to the first rocky outcropping (at about 800 feet) and pause for the view. This is especially pretty in autumn when the birch-aspen forest covering the Resurrection Creek valley is a brilliant gold. Plan on a 15-minute stroll along the stream and another ½ hour to reach the outcropping. To this point the trip is suitable for most children.

At the outcropping the hiker is essentially above timberline and only his physical conditioning limits him in the steep hike up the ridge above. Follow the crest of the ridge up to a point where you can plan your route to the top of Hope Point, 3708 feet. The easiest is the mossy slope with southern exposure.

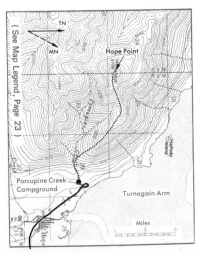

Devil's Club, August (Photo by Nancy Simmerman)

Turnagain Arm from ridge below Hope Point, October (Photo by Nancy Simmerman)

On the way up there are sweeping views of Turnagain Arm and the mountains rimming it and of Cook Inlet and Fire Island. Note the speed of the tide as it goes in and out. Watch for a bore tide, a wall of water on the incoming tide. There is no drinking water after Porcupine Creek and no wood up high. The ridge is grass and moss with scrub hemlock and a few alder on the shoulder. Crowberries, bearberries, caribou moss, and ground cedar cover the slope to the summit. Moose and bear droppings are abundant so watch for the animals themselves.

From Hope Point the hiker can ridge walk to the south as far as he desires. Lack of water is the most limiting factor, although early in the summer snowdrifts can provide some. Plan to spend as much time as possible in this alpine wonderland as there are other ridges to explore after reaching Hope Point.

KENAI PENINSULA

17 Gull Rock

Round trip 9 miles
Hiking time 5-7 hours
High point 700 feet
Elevation gain 620 feet
Best May—October
USGS map Seward D8
Chugach National Forest

A delightful walk along the southwest side of Turnagain Arm with a very gentle gradient. Views of the Arm and the Chugach Mountains east of McHugh Peak. Enjoy the smell and sound of the water. Watch for moose on land, beluga whales in the water. An easy trail, good for hikers of any age who can walk 9 miles round trip.

The trail to Gull Rock leaves from the Hope area and parallels Turnagain Arm for 4½ miles. It is an old wagon road which has been overgrown in parts and recently brushed out by the Forest Service. At present the trail is cleared only to Gull Rock, but long-range plans call for eventual extension along the shoreline farther west to the Chickaloon flats. The old wagon trail does go beyond Gull Rock but is not brushed out; it meets a bulldozer track a few miles to the west where the natural gas pipeline crosses Turnagain Arm. The pipeline and cat track come from the Kenai area.

Drive to mile 56.3 on the Seward Highway (68 miles south of Anchorage). Here turn north onto the 17-mile gravel side-road leading to Hope. Go around Hope and continue another mile to the road's end at the Chugach National Forest Porcupine Creek Campground. The trail leaves from the far (northwestern) end of the campground.

Beginning at an elevation of about 80 feet, the trail winds along the shoreline well above tidewater, reaching an elevation of 700 feet at one point before it drops back down to Gull Rock at 140 feet. The way is never steep. Breaks in the trees afford views of the Arm and shoreline. The variety of vegetation through which the trail passes is fascinating: from pleasant birch-aspen woods to alder-choked gullies, to young conifer forests, to an open section where the growth can only be described as above-timberline plantlife, with tiny spruce, mosses, lichens, low cranberry bushes, and saxifrages, thence into stately hemlock forest carpeted by deep moss under the trees. The trail passes moss- and lichen-covered rock faces conveniently located for investigating the interesting plants. At one point the trail crosses an avalanche gully so steep and straight that it looks like a suicidal bobsled run, ending in the tidewater of Turnagain Arm.

Equally fascinating are the reminders of earlier days: bits of old corduroy roadbed, the remains of a cabin and stable on Johnson Creek near the end of the trail, an old

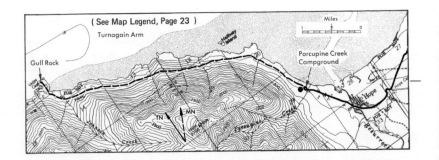

Turnagain Arm from Gull Rock, November (Photo by Nancy Simmerman)

but still sturdy bridge across the creek, ruins of a sawmill a little farther on. The wagon road was built in the late 1920s, probably originally as a fire trail.

Continue on the trail to the rocky promontory of Gull Rock. Sit and listen to the turbulent water swirl around the rocks below as the tides flow in and out. Just above Turnagain Arm on the other side, a tiny stream of cars flows by. McHugh Creek Picnic Site is directly across the Arm.

There is plenty of water along the trail but few good camping spots. Fires should be built only on bare dirt or rock, not on peat or moss. The best camping is at Porcupine Creek Campground.

KENAI PENINSULA

18 Turnagain Pass Ski Tour

Round trip 6½ miles
Skiing time 4-10 hours
High point 2200 feet
Elevation gain 1250 feet
Best November—April
USGS map Seward D6
Chugach National Forest

A delightful winter ski or snowshoe tour in one of the few places closed to snow-mobiles. Beautiful winter mountain scenery in an area generally noted for lots of deep, light, fluffy snow, a real winter playground for the ski or snowshoe enthusiast, with the added benefit of silence, the way winter was meant to be. Watch for wolverine, rabbits, eagles, and tree squirrels. The U.S. Forest Service sometimes flags the trail for winter use and eventually plans to clear a summer hiking trail in this area.

Drive to mile 68.3 on the Seward Highway (59 miles south of Anchorage) where there is a large sign denoting Turnagain Pass winter sports area. Park in the large area provided on the west side of the highway (elevation about 950 feet). The Forest Service has designated the west side of the highway for snowmobiles and the east side for skiers and snowshoers. Outhouses are provided at the parking area.

Cross the road and, on skis or snowshoes, parallel the highway south about ¼ mile, skirting the knobs and ridge. Cross the first creek, Tincan, and, leaving the highway, follow the south bank of the creek upstream to the powerline. At the first power pole south of Tincan Creek, head up the valley to the east, through the conifer forest. The route winds gently uphill, through natural clearings, first paralleling Tincan Creek, then swinging south to parallel Lyon Creek. Snow hangs heavily on the trees, creating a myriad of imaginary giants and monsters.

Even a short trip winding through these snow-laden trees is an excursion into the best Alaska's winters have to offer. Timberline, at about 1500 feet elevation and about 1½ miles from the parking lot, makes a good destination for a short day.

Once through the timber, there is a broad expanse of open snow with Lyon Creek nearby to the south. Head north, away from Lyon Creek, climbing up an obvious bowl to the crest of the low ridge which separates Tincan and Lyon Creeks. Traverse the north side of the higher knobs and follow the ridge crest as far as desired. Jagged white mountain ridges rise all around, making this an unforgettable winter experience.

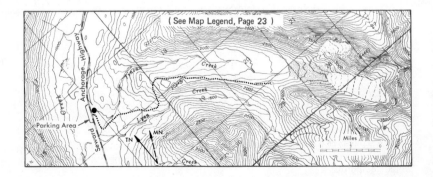

(See Map Legend, Page 23)

66

Lyon Creek Valley and the "low ridge" (Photo by Nancy Simmerman)

In midwinter the sun seldom reaches the low ridge or the valleys beyond, so dress warmly. Fortunately, wind is unusual here. Stay on the ridge to avoid avalanche hazard on the side slopes of the higher peaks and on the valley floor. (See "Avalanches," page 17.)

Even now (before the Forest Service begins to clear and mark a trail) summer hiking up Lyon Creek is attractive, as the brush can be circumvented. A good game trail on the center ridge leads to high country.

Portage Glacier, July – Way No. 21 (Photo by Nancy Simmerman)

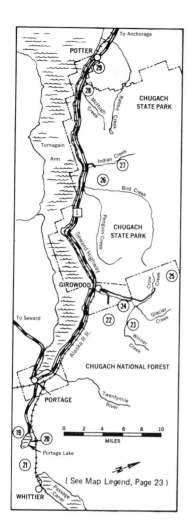

POTTER TO PORTAGE

19 Byron Glacier View

Round trip 1½ miles
Hiking time ½-1 hour
High point 280 feet
Elevation gain 100 feet
Best May—October
USGS map Seward D5
Chugach National Forest

In summer this is a delightful walk for families with small children, for Aunt Minnie, and spry great-grandmother. There is essentially no climbing. The trail is wide and smooth, and the view from the end of the trail is exciting for those who have never seen rugged mountain and glacier terrain up close. This is hiking in the heart of snow-and-ice country without any effort or danger.

From Portage at mile 79 on the Seward Highway (49 miles south of Anchorage) drive the 5-mile side-road east to Portage Glacier Recreational Area. At the Portage Glacier Lodge take the right-hand fork of the paved road, and continue bearing right to the end about 1 mile from the lodge. Park here.

Follow the marked trail to the view of Byron Peak and Glacier. The alders along the pathway make wonderful horses for young children to ride. Byron Creek, along the last half of the trail, is handy for throwing stones into, and the vast quantities of stream-washed stones build into tottering towers and fortresses. Usually a large bank of snow remains near the end of the trail—a remnant of the avalanches which swept across the valley the winter before. Great for snowfights. Note the areas of ice not connected with the glacier; these are left by the glacier as it retreats up the valley. Bring a picnic lunch and relax here.

Although the summer temperature may be cooler than in Anchorage, the Byron Glacier valley is protected from the icy winds that blow from Portage Glacier. Here the sun is warm. For camping, plan to use one of the excellent Forest Service campgrounds you passed on the 5-mile road leading to Portage Glacier viewpoint.

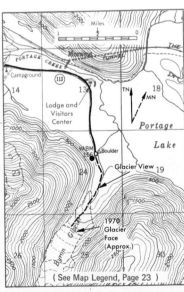

(See Map Legend, Page 23)

Broomrape, July (Photo by Nancy Simmerman)

Byron Peak and Glacier from end of trail, June (Photo by Nancy Simmerman)

Water is available during the summer season. The Portage Glacier Lodge and Chugach National Forest Visitors' Center both close for the winter after Labor Day and do not reopen until Memorial Day.

If the trip is taken in winter do not go into the valley because of high avalanche hazard. Go just far enough for a view. (See "Avalanches," page 17.) In any season, travel onto the glacier is for experienced and properly equipped mountaineers only. Do not venture into ice caves or near towering ice faces. They can and do collapse.

This trail is closed to motorized uses year-round and to horses April 1 to June 30.

POTTER TO PORTAGE

20 Portage Lake Ski Tour

Round trip 4½ miles
Skiing time 1-3 hours
High point 150 feet
Elevation gain none
Best December—March
USGS map Seward D5
Chugach National Forest

An easy winter ski tour across Portage Lake into terrain unavailable at any other time of year. Closeup views of the ice cliffs of Portage Glacier. Good for snowshoes, too, or just for walking, as the ice is often windswept clear.

At mile 79 on the Seward Highway (49 miles south of Anchorage) take the 5-mile paved side-road to Portage Glacier, and park in the area provided for viewing the glacier.

Make sure the ice on Portage Lake is strong enough, then chart the course toward the ice cliffs of Portage Glacier, and go. Make detours, of course, to investigate the strange and beautiful amorphous shapes of last summer's icebergs, now frozen in place. Take pictures of the weird forms and admire the intense blue of the ice. Climbing on the icebergs is tempting but dangerous as they do break loose and topple over. Lake ice may be thin at the base of the icebergs.

Continue on for a look at the ice cliffs rising 75 to 100 feet high. Those inexperienced in glacier travel should stay ¼ mile away from the glacier face. The frozen lake surface gives a deceptive appearance of safety. Glacier activity continues throughout the winter, and chunks of ice may break away from the ice cliffs at any time. This, of course, is a hazard in itself, but it can also create cracks in the lake ice which may then be bridged over by thin ice and snow. Flat light or whiteout conditions make these bridged cracks hard to see, even for the experienced.

Portage Glacier is retreating at an average rate of 50 to 75 feet per year. In 1969, however, the southern edge of the glacier receded 180 feet and the northern edge 500 feet. In 1970, although the north side remained basically unchanged, the south side retreated about 435 feet. This activity is the cause of the numerous icebergs in the lake. The lake depth averages 400 to 450 feet but is 600 feet at its deepest point.

Wear warm clothes since the Portage area is often windy, but don't let an overcast day cancel the trip. The colors of the ice seem more intense on cloudy days, and the weather is definitely warmer. Portage Glacier Lodge does not remain open in the

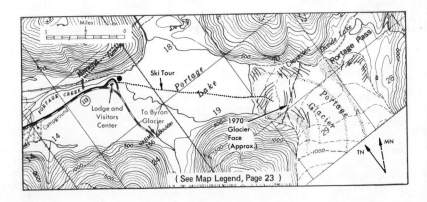

72

Portage Lake and Glacier, March (Photo by Nancy Simmerman)

winter nor does the Chugach National Forest Visitors' Center. The nearest warmth and food are at Portage on the Seward Highway.

The road between the parking lot at the lodge and Byron Glacier is the boundary between the snowmobile area (west of the road) and the cross-country ski area (the lake area, east of the road).

21 Portage Pass

**Round trip 5.2 miles to viewpoint;
7.2 miles to glacier
Hiking time 4-7 hours
High point 750 feet
Elevation gain 750 feet
Best July—September
USGS map Seward D5
Chugach National Forest**

Hop the train to Whittier, prepared for an easy uphill hike, good for all ages, with spectacular views of Portage Glacier, Passage Canal, and surrounding mountains. The strategic location of Portage Pass, on the isthmus between Turnagain Arm and ice-free Passage Canal, gave it an historic role. Hundreds of years ago Indians and Russians used it as a trading route. Following the discovery of gold in the Turnagain Arm area, Alaska's first gold rush began in 1896. Prospectors used Portage Pass and Glacier as a winter route to this area. Portage Pass is also a major route for migrating birds, including arctic terns, sandhill cranes, swans, ducks and geese.

The Alaska Railroad runs an inexpensive summer shuttle from Anchorage and Portage to Whittier. Cars may be taken on the train if space is available. Call the Alaska Railroad for information.

Drive toward Portage to about Seward Highway mile 80.4, approximately 48 miles south of Anchorage. Foot passengers park in the north area; those taking cars on the train follow the signs for ferry traffic.

The train goes through two tunnels before reaching Whittier. The trail starts near the second tunnel exit, but the train continues about 1 mile farther. After leaving the Alaska Railroad ramp, turn 180° and walk or drive the gravel road which heads west paralleling the tracks. Continue on this road almost to the tank farm near the tunnel. Take the only road which goes left across the tracks. Find a convenient parking place. The road beyond this point is better traveled on foot.

Follow the right fork of the road past the shell of a white house; go right at the next branch and continue up the steep old road. At the pass, the trees are left behind and the old road disappears into a little pond. This is a fine picnic spot. Bear right on the trail to a promontory (elevation 750 feet) for a view of Portage Glacier. Burns Glacier can be seen emerging from the left-most valley and butting against Portage Glacier; it used to flow through Portage Pass, on the rebound from hitting Portage Glacier.

To reach the glacier, a mile away, descend through brush, following gravel patches when possible, to Divide Lake. Go around the lakeshore to the left to the lake's true

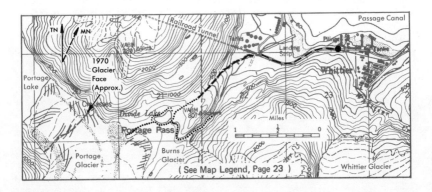

(See Map Legend, Page 23)

Burns and Portage Glaciers, July (Photo by Nancy Simmerman)

outlet. Follow the stream to the glacier. Total elevation loss is about 200 feet.

Divide Lake now drains toward the glacier, not to Whittier as the USGS map indicates. The change may be due to the 1964 earthquake. With the current rate of stream-cutting at the new outlet the lake may be drained within a few years. The streambed of the old outlet now provides good exploring; follow it to a narrow canyon.

Water and campsites are available at the pass. Carrying a mountain stove is advisable, although some scrub willow is available. Watch the weather carefully as Portage Pass can be a wind funnel, although wind at Whittier, particularly from the west, does not always mean wind at the pass. Whittier has the second highest precipitation level in Alaska (annual total 175.28 inches). The greatest snow depth measured in Whittier was 141 inches; at the pass it can be as much as 250 inches or more. Although low in elevation, snow often remains in the pass through June.

POTTER TO PORTAGE

22 Alyeska Glacier View

Via chairlift round trip ⅔ mile
Hiking time 1-2 hours
High point 2750 feet
Elevation gain 310 feet
Best June—September
USGS map Seward D6

Via foot round trip 3 miles
Hiking time 3-5 hours
High point 2750 feet
Elevation gain 2410 feet
Best June—September
USGS map Seward D6
Chugach National Forest

A beautiful view of Turnagain Arm and the Girdwood Valley. Possibilities range from an easy romp with the children to technical mountaineering. The trip described is a short uphill walk to a viewpoint, but many will want to go on to the summit of Mt. Alyeska at 3939 feet. Frequently visitors sight marmots and mountain goats. Skiing is often possible on the glacier and upper parts of the mountain through June.

At mile 90 on the Seward Highway (35 miles south of Anchorage) turn north on a paved road, following signs to Mt. Alyeska Resort and park.

It is the chairlift which makes this an easy outing. During the summer the lift is operated every afternoon. (Check with Alyeska Resort for rates and schedule.) From the top of the chairlift, at 2540 feet, climb the knob above the sun deck, and continue up the ridge to a view of tiny Alyeska Glacier (elevation of viewpoint about 2750 feet). Relax, play, picnic, soak up the view here on the heather-covered mountainsides. Join the children in sliding down the steep slopes or glissading on snow patches. Be sure to find out when the chairlift closes.

Hikers who feel that chairlifts are an unethical way to reach timberline can certainly walk! From the ski lodge, at 340 feet, look for the tracked-vehicle trail which climbs the ski slope on the south side of Alyeska Creek, paralleling the canyon. This leads to the sun deck at the top of the chairlift. An alternate route begins on the tracked-vehicle trail but, halfway to the sun deck, turns left and crosses the creek at the head of the canyon. Follow this route to mid-station on the chairlift. From there follow a trail up the ski slope to the sun deck and on to the view of Alyeska Glacier.

A popular approach to the viewpoint is to ride the chairlift up and walk back down. To descend, follow the trail from the sun deck into the bowl, across Alyeska Creek,

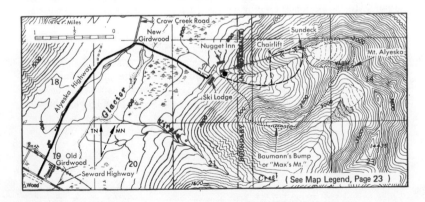

Alyeska Glacier, July (Photo by Nancy Simmerman)

and down the mountain. Or walk the slope under the chairlift to mid-station, then take the higher tracked-vehicle trail to the left to join the bowl trail.

The more adventurous may wish to climb Mt. Alyeska. Two routes are possible: (1) continue up the ridge you followed to view the glacier; (2) from the sun deck drop down to cross Alyeska Creek and climb the center ridge which begins near the creek in the bowl. Both routes have exposed spots where the novice may prefer a rope belay. Descend by either route, or follow the southwest ridge around the bowl to point 3302, officially Baumann's Bump, locally known as "Max's Mountain." No trail exists down Max's, but the descent is not difficult; from point 3302 bear due west to avoid cliffs, then descend to a bench covered with low vegetation. Follow this to the right until an opening appears in the alders and continue downward through it to the ski slope. Walking the ski slope may be a bit unpleasant because of vegetation until the tracked-vehicle trail is reached. Allow 3 to 6 hours from the top of the chair to the summit of Mt. Alyeska and down by this route, a distance of about 5 miles.

In season salmonberries and blueberries can be found along these trails. There is no water up high and Alyeska Creek is silty, so carry water. Climbing on the glacier and the ridge traverse to point 4435 should be attempted only by experienced mountaineers.

POTTER TO PORTAGE

23 Winner Creek

Gorge round trip 7 miles
Hiking time 4-6 hours
High point 550 feet
Elevation gain 210 feet
Best May—October
USGS map Seward D6

Trail round trip 18 miles
Allow 2 days
High point 2855 feet
Elevation gain 2515 feet
Best June—October
USGS map Seward D6

Ski system round trip 1⅔ to 6⅔ miles
Skiing time 1-6 hours
High point 550 feet
Elevation gain 210 feet
Best November—April
USGS map Seward D6
Chugach National Forest

A lovely trip in the area at the base of Mt. Alyeska, offering a variety of possibilities. In winter the trail offers excellent cross-country skiing. In summer take a pleasant 1-day woodland stroll to Winner Creek gorge or a longer 2-day trip up Winner Creek to timberline and view country. Really energetic (and experienced) hikers can continue to the headwaters of Winner Creek from which there is access to Twentymile country and other intriguing areas.

At mile 90 on the Seward Highway (35 miles south of Anchorage) turn north on a paved road, following signs for Alyeska Resort. Follow the pavement to the Alyeska Nugget Inn and park.

Walk to the north end of the Inn, past the upper condominiums and cross under the rope tow. The trailhead is marked. In winter this is an entrance to the cross-country ski trail system. The trail, starting at 340 feet elevation, wanders through mature hemlock and spruce forest. Ferns, blueberry bushes, and moss carpet the summer forest floor. The Forest Service plans to mark and improve both the summer hiking trail and the winter ski trails. Until then, follow the pink ribbons marking the hiking trail for the most direct route. The trail crosses pleasant creeks, and short sections of wet muskeg.

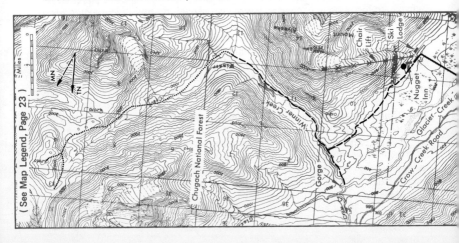

(See Map Legend, Page 23)

Winner Creek gorge, August (Photo by Nancy Simmerman)

About 2½ miles from Alyeska the flagged trail intersects two NE-SW trails. Continue to the second such intersection which is on the side of the steep wooded canyon of Winner Creek. The left branch goes to Winner Creek gorge, less than a mile away, and is well worth the walk. The right branch leads up Winner Creek about 5 miles to brushline, wandering through meadows, alder, willow patches, and cottonwood forest. Approximately the first 2 miles of the trail have been cleared; beyond the first tributary on the right it may be necessary to wade in the stream occasionally to avoid brush. Eventually this part of the trail will also be cut. After that the trail has been cleared to brushline at about 1500 feet. Good walking from there on to point 2855 at the head of the valley or beyond.

Except for the upper reaches of Winner Creek, the trails are gentle with no severe ups and downs. Wear waterproof boots. Water is regularly available along both trails, but between Alyeska and the gorge there is no convenient camping spot. However, upper Winner Creek has many tempting tent sites with water and view. Watch for moose and possibly bear. The upper Winner Creek trail is not recommended in winter because of high avalanche hazard. (See "Avalanches," page 17.)

The wintertime ski trail consists of three connecting loops, (2½ km., 5 km., and 10 km.) utilizing parts of the first 2 miles of the summer hiking trail. In winter follow the track set by previous skiers, skiing the loops counterclockwise, and taking care not to destroy the center ridge between the ski tracks. Please, no feet, snowshoes, or snowmobiles on the ski trail because they destroy the trail for skiing.

This trail is closed to all motorized uses and to horses from April 1 through June 30.

POTTER TO PORTAGE

24 Glacier Creek Ski Tour

Round trip up to 12 miles
Skiing time 3-10 hours
High point 800 feet
Elevation gain 650 feet
Best December—February
USGS maps Seward D6, Anchorage A6
Chugach National Forest

A lovely midwinter ski tour up Glacier Creek near Girdwood, through magnificent winter scenery. Because the stream surface is smooth and level this is an excellent trip for beginners. Good for snowshoes, too, but dangerous on foot or snowmobile because of potential thin ice pockets.

From mile 90 on the Seward Highway (35 miles south of Anchorage) turn north on the paved road leading to Alyeska and Girdwood. 2¼ miles from the Seward Highway turn left just before the bridge onto Hightower Drive and continue north past the Post Office and trailer court, winding along the gravel road until reaching the Girdwood elementary school. Park here.

On skis or snowshoes head down the stream bank and onto Glacier Creek ice. Follow the stream bed upvalley, to the north, avoiding any open channels in the creek. Certain portions of the creek near here, and near the Alyeska Highway bridge, seldom freeze over, while the canyon section of the creek will be perfectly passable. So give the route a try before deciding it is not possible.

Follow the stream bed through Glacier Creek canyon, noting the entry of Winner Creek from the right and Crow Creek from the left about 3 miles from the start. This is a beautiful trip, giving the skier a river's-eye view of a canyon. Note the lovely hoarfrost crystals growing in the ice caverns above the open water. Continue up Glacier Creek, beyond the entry of Crow Creek, to the narrows, the most scenic part of the canyon. Beyond the narrows is the beautiful valley of Glacier Creek's headwaters, with hanging glaciers and snowy peaks all around. Continue as far as time, temperature, and snow conditions permit.

Dress warmly; the route is in the bottom of a canyon where sun seldom reaches at this time of year. A thermos of hot bouillon hits the spot at rest time on the trail. Be cautious of thin ice. Test questionable spots first with a ski pole, then with a hard stamp of the foot. Generally the depth of the water beneath you is not great. This trip is suggested only for the coldest months because the weather must be cold enough for Glacier Creek to freeze solidly. On skis or snowshoes weight is so well distributed that

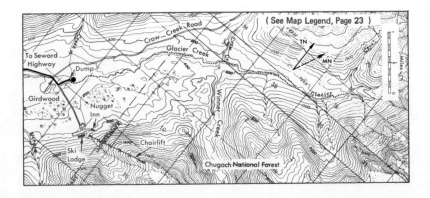

Glacier Creek canyon, January (Photo by Nancy Simmerman)

the danger of breaking through the ice is slight. If a ski trail is already established snowshoers should make their own trail when space permits. Snowshoes break down the center ridge between ski tracks, eliminating the advantage of a prepared trail.

Glacier Creek is closed at all times to motorized vehicles.

POTTER TO PORTAGE

25 Crow Pass

Round trip 8 miles; traverse 20 miles
Hiking time 4-6 hours; traverse 3-4 days
High point 3500 feet
Elevation gain 1950 feet
Best mid-June—early October
Winter: extremely hazardous
USGS maps Anchorage A6, A7
Chugach National Forest
Chugach State Park

A fine trail for experienced hikers, traversing a beautiful mountain wilderness area. One can see gold mine ruins, view glaciers, picnic by an alpine lake, identify many Alaska wildflowers, have the excitement of fording mountain streams, and walk a dogsled route once traveled by mail carriers, explorers, and prospectors.

In the early 1900s the trail over Crow Pass was part of the Iditarod winter dogsled trail through the mountains between Turnagain and Knik Arms, en route from Seward to Knik, thence to interior gold fields. It was used alternately with the Indian Pass trail (Trip 27), the preferred trail. Steady use of both trails probably ended in the early 1920s when regular railroad service began between Seward and Fairbanks.

The old mail trail continued from Crow Pass down Raven Creek and out Eagle River. Trail work has opened up an excellent 3-4 day trip. River crossings and uncertain trail maintenance make allowing 4 days advisable. Contact the Chugach State Park office for current information.

At mile 90 of the Seward Highway (35 miles south of Anchorage) turn north on a paved road leading to Mt. Alyeska resort. Stay on this road for 2 miles. As the paved road rounds a curve to the right, turn to the left onto Crow Creek Road, a gravel road with signs advertising the Erickson Gold Mine. Continue 5½ miles to the road's end and park just past the last bridge, at an elevation of 1550 feet. Expect no winter maintenance beyond the first ½ mile of Crow Creek Road.

Continue on foot up the trail, leaving the tree line behind. At 1.7 miles from the parking area (elevation 2500 feet) are the Girdwood Mine ruins, a successful hard-rock gold mine from 1906-1948. The trail passes remains of mills and crew's quarters; above in the cliffs are mine shafts. Walk uphill behind the mine ruins for a side-trip along the flume into the beautiful canyon through which Crow Creek cascades.

To reach Crow Pass follow the steep trail above the mine toward the pass. At 3450 feet, 3 miles from the parking area, is an A-frame built by the Forest Service for public use. (Make reservations with the Chugach National Forest office.)

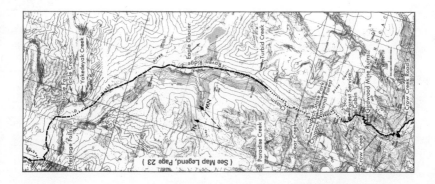

(See Map Legend, Page 23)

Crow Pass cabin and Crystal Lake, August (Photo by Nancy Simmerman)

The cabin is a splendid enough destination for many. Nearby Crystal Lake, nestled beneath a mountain, is rimmed by wildflowers in July. To the right of the lake is the tip of Crow Glacier. Go past the cabin and through the pass to visit Raven Glacier, about a mile farther. Look for Dall sheep and mountain goats.

Camping spots abound in both the mine and pass areas. Water is available, but campfires are not allowed anywhere in Chugach State Park. Snow showers and strong winds are probable anytime, so take a parka, cap, and mittens. The trail is highly hazardous in winter because of avalanche danger. (See "Avalanches," p. 17.)

From the Raven Glacier overlook follow the trail along the moraine bench on the southwestern side of Raven Glacier for about a mile. Walk down the hill toward a big gravel bar, staying on the west side of Raven Creek until reaching the gravel bar. Cross Clear Creek at its junction with Raven Creek (easy crossing). In ½ mile cross

Raven Creek on a bridge at the lower end of the gravel bar and just above a gorge. Note the natural stone arch at the bottom of the waterfall in the gorge. From this point bear sightings are frequent.

The trail now parallels the east side of Raven Creek for about 3 miles, staying on the hillside above it. In a mile is Turbid Creek, narrow but swift and boiling, difficult to cross when high. Remove your pack, throw it across, then boulder hop. A bridge is planned here. Clear drinking water is not likely to be available in this stretch. At times the trail lies on the historic trailbed and at times parallel to it. Where the trail appears to be coming out onto Raven Ridge, leave the trail and climb the ridge for a view of Eagle Glacier.

During June through August the old fording area for Eagle River has become very hazardous because of high run-off, so a new crossing has been marked by flagging. (This can be seen from the ridge with binoculars, about a mile steeply down.) The crossing is signed and mapped, with instructions on how to ford.

After the crossing, the new trail follows the river bank for about 1½ miles. Thunder Falls is reached at about 1.0 mile. The subsequent stretch of trail, traversing the cliff close to the river, is potentially hazardous because of danger of erosion and high water. **It is important to check with Chugach State Park staff about current conditions before beginning the trip.** Following the new trail, it is about 4.5 miles to Icicle Creek from the river crossing, and about 9 miles to Paradise Haven and the trail's end.

In 1976 an area between Yakedeyak Creek and Dew Mound was burned in a forest fire, started by a campfire. It burned for 60 days and cost over $500,000 to fight. Dead trees continue to blow down, making caution necessary on a windy day.

Several minor stream crossings in this stretch mean probable wet feet. All are easy, but Icicle Creek has numerous branches. The route parallels Eagle River and crosses the braids of Icicle Creek. Look for trail markers. The trail continues across Dishwater Creek and past a raspberry patch (watch for bears here in berry season) to connect with Dew Mound Trail (Trip 38). Many good campsites are to be found along the way, but campfires are prohibited.

A copy of the topographic map showing the trail is available for viewing at the Chugach State Park office. The entire trail is closed to motorized vehicles. The portion in the Chugach National Forest is closed to horses from April 1 to June 30.

Crow Glacier and Crow Pass (Photo by Nancy Simmerman)

26 Bird Ridge

Round trip 4¼ miles
Hiking time 3-6 hours
High point 3505 feet
Elevation gain 3500 feet
Best April—October
USGS maps Anchorage A7, Seward D7
Chugach State Park.

One of the best and earliest spring hikes because of its southern exposure. Beautiful views of fjordlike Turnagain Arm. Steep, but worth it! Take a picnic lunch in the spring, climb as high as desired, stretch out on the ground, and enjoy the sunshine and smell of earth while all other mountains around remain cloaked in white. A good early-spring conditioner. Excellent winter hiking on the ridge, but stay on the ridge crest to avoid avalanches. (See "Avalanches," page 17.)

Drive to Bird Creek at mile 101.4 on the Seward Highway (26.5 miles south of Anchorage). Park on either side of the bridge in the areas provided. Bird Ridge is on the west side of the stream. The trail is marked.

The hike begins almost at sea level. Do not follow the trail along the creek bank. Take the left fork which climbs the ridge to the powerline. At the powerline follow the cut about 60 feet to the left (northwest) watching for the footpath which leaves the powerline cut and continues upward. Soon the hiker is above brush and can follow the ridge to the first high point, 3505 feet. In early spring it may be necessary to skirt snow patches still remaining on the ridge crest. The hiker with time and energy can continue over point 3505 to any of the various high points on the ridge beyond. The ridge eventually culminates 7 miles away at 4960 feet overlooking the headwaters of Ship Creek.

Whether the hiker reaches point 3505 or stops at the powerline (elevation about 400 feet) the view of the surrounding mountains and of Turnagain Arm is magnificent. Turnagain was so named by Captain James Cook in 1778 when he explored these waters as part of his search for the Northwest Passage. Turnagain Arm has one of the world's greatest tide differentials with a range of as much as 33 feet. The Arm, which was scoured out by ice, has since been filled by material which streams carry down from the retreating glaciers. At low tide these mud flats are clearly visible and only the river and stream channels still carry water. Because of the speed of the tide as it pours into and out of the narrow Arm, and because of frequent high winds, the waters are dangerous for small boats.

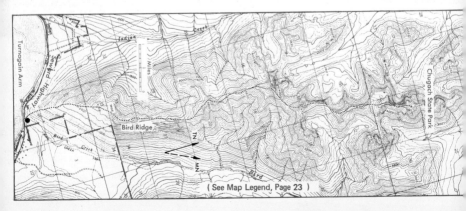

(See Map Legend, Page 23)

Bird Ridge, May (Photo by Ginny Hill Wood)

The first wildflowers of the season can be found on Bird Ridge, starting with Jacob's ladder and anemones in the early spring and continuing with the whole cycle of dry tundra plants. Hikers may, in early spring or fall, see a ptarmigan in the process of changing color. The footing is excellent, the hike steep in spots, but not unpleasantly so. There is no water along the ridge. The best camping is at Bird Creek Campground several hundred feet east of Bird Creek bridge. Campfires are permitted only in Bird Creek Campground.

POTTER TO PORTAGE

27 Indian Valley

Round trip 12 miles; traverse 21 miles
Hiking time 7 hours; traverse 3 days
High point 2350 feet
Elevation gain 2100 feet
Best May—October; winter: February—March
USGS maps Anchorage A7, Seward D7
Chugach State Park

Indian Valley offers a good family hike from May to October with a delightful combination of forest, meadows, mountains, stream, and lakes. The trail, worn by use, is marked but not regularly maintained. In the early 1900s this was a winter dogsled trail from Indian to Ship Creek, part of the Iditarod trail from Seward to interior gold fields, used alternately with Crow Pass trail (Trip 25). The Indian Creek part has been marked and brushed out. The entire trip can be made in winter on snowshoes or skis; the trip up Indian Valley itself makes a good 1-day winter trip. The route crosses several avalanche runouts.

Indian Creek Pass, April (Photo by Dick Mize)

Drive the Seward Highway to about mile 103 (25 miles south of Sears in Anchorage) and turn left on the first major road east of Indian Road, just before a restaurant and shortly before Indian Creek. After ½ mile take the right fork and continue to the end. Park in the area provided.

Continue on foot. The trailhead is marked and follows part of the old Iditarod trail. The trail can be wet, so shoepacs or well-greased boots are advisable. Follow the marked trail through spruce woods. Occasional delightful meadows are crossed, created by winter avalanches (beware of these open places in winter during periods of high avalanche danger. (See "Avalanches," page 17.) Plan to ford a creek 4 miles from the trailhead. The terrain changes gradually from timber to alder to tundra; the climb is very gentle.

The pass offers ideal camping but not until June. Water is plentiful but bring a stove as there are no campfires permitted. The pass is an old moraine, its knobs and dips well-vegetated with scrub hemlock and crowberry bushes. Many inviting trips beckon up nearby ridges, into side-valleys, and up to little lakes. (See Trip 32, "Ship Lake.")

Hikers can continue over the pass and 15 miles out Ship Creek, though there is no marked trail. There are swamps and brush lower down. Traces of the old trail can still be found. Ruins of a roadhouse are on the west side of Ship Creek, about a mile above its confluence with North Fork Ship Creek. Look for a tank trail on the east side of lower Ship Creek 9 or 10 miles from Indian Pass. In winter the trip is usually made beginning from the Ship Creek end on the tank road at the Anchorage watershed sign on Arctic Valley Ski Bowl Road. The 21-mile trip will take 3 days if it is necessary to break trail, though strong skiers can make it in 1 long day in spring if conditions are ideal. Take USGS Anchorage A7 map to avoid confusion at the north fork of Ship Creek. With a heavy pack the fast descent from Indian Pass to Indian can be difficult for the novice skier. Do not attempt the Powerline Pass trail (see Trip 32) in winter due to extreme avalanche hazard. Check avalanche and trail conditions with Alaska Division of Parks, Chugach District (phone 271-4500).

The area is closed to all motorized vehicles.

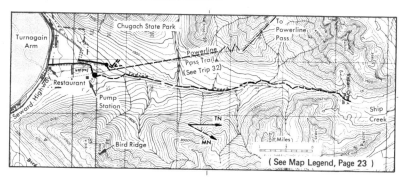

28 Table Rock and Beyond

Round trip 2 miles
Hiking time 1-2 hours
High point 1100 feet
Elevation gain 1000 feet
Best April—October
USGS map Anchorage A8
Chugach State Park

One of the nicest early-spring hikes, though steep in places. Snow is gone early from this south-facing slope, and the lower part of the hike can often be done as early as April. Wildflowers abound and are in bloom by mid-May. Brilliant autumn colors. Tree squirrels, rabbits, and birds are likely to be seen—possibly also parka (ground) squirrels and moose. The lower part of the trail passes through lovely woods of spruce, birch, and cottonwood. Views of Turnagain Arm are spectacular. The hike to Table Rock is good for children used to hiking uphill. Footgear with good traction is desirable. The trail, at present merely a well-worn foot track, is slippery when wet. Beyond Table Rock the hike becomes very steep and in one place is a rock scramble. No water is available.

From Sears in Anchorage, at Northern Lights Boulevard and the Seward Highway, drive south on Seward Highway about 14 miles to McHugh Creek Picnic Site. Follow the entrance road and take the left fork to the upper parking lot. Park here. On foot, follow the Old Johnson Trail (marked) a short distance. Where it turns left, take instead an inconspicuous trail to the right. Follow this trail along the base of the mountain to the bank above McHugh Creek.

The trail begins the steep uphill climb here. Go right around 3 magnificent old spruce. As the trail climbs, it veers away from the stream to the north (left). Soon after the ascent begins, the trail climbs over a rock outcropping.

Jacob's ladder, lupine, violets, highbush cranberry, bearberry, columbine, wild geranium, dwarf dogwood, wild rose, pyrola, and other wildflowers grace the trailside. Delightful rocky promontories lure the hiker to rest on calm days. (Wind should not be a deterrent from the hike as it is not a problem in the woods.) Beyond the first rocky promontory the trail forks in several places. Keep bearing left. After climbing through forest for ½ to 1 hour the trail veers left and is briefly level. Watch for a left fork to a

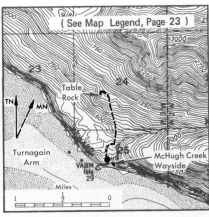

(See Map Legend, Page 23)

Cow parsnip, July (Photo by Nancy Simmerman)

Turnagain Arm and Resurrection Creek Valley from trail, September (Photo by Pete Martin)

windswept rocky outcrop known as Table Rock. The view of the inlet and mountains beyond is superb.

This is destination enough for a picnic or evening. But the hiker can continue to the ridge above. With a little searching in places he can find a trail through all the brush. Leaving Table Rock the trail is obvious, continuing very steeply upwards through woods, eventually leading to an almost vertical and narrow dirt track up between cliffs. This is not technical climbing, but it is necessary to pull oneself up in spots with the aid of rocks and trees. Test the holds before using them! Once above the cliffs follow the now sometimes hard-to-find trail through natural clearings and bands of cottonwood trees. If the trail disappears, pick the easiest route. Upon leaving timber, note the surroundings and line them up with landmarks below to assist in finding the way back to the lower trail. After reaching brushline pick your own route and destination. Allow 5-7 hours round trip to the ridge.

Horses and sledge on the Old Johnson Trail, from an early photo (Photo courtesy The Alaska Railroad)

POTTER TO PORTAGE

29 Old Johnson Trail

One way 11 miles
Hiking time 8-11 hours
High point 900 feet
Elevation gain 900 feet
Best April—November
USGS maps Anchorage A8, Seward D7, D8
Chugach State Park

A mountain goat's eye view of Turnagain Arm. A scenic stroll to find the first wildflowers of spring. Watch for bore tides, mountain goats and Dall sheep, beluga whales. The trail predates Anchorage and was used as an alternate mail trail from Seward to Knik when snow conditions permitted. The main trails went over Crow Pass (Trip 25) and Indian Valley (Trip 27).

Take the Seward Highway to Potter (1) (milepost 115, 10.7 miles south of Sears in Anchorage). Just beyond the old Potter railroad section house, turn left up a steep dirt road to the first switchback. Park off the road. In winter park in the pull-off across the Seward Highway and walk to the first switchback. The trailhead is marked. In spring portions of the trail are wet. McHugh Creek is 3½ miles to the east.

At McHugh Creek Picnic Site (2), follow the paved road to the parking lot beside the creek. Take the trail up the left side of the creek, and cross the bridge. Just beyond the first switchback, an inconspicuous, but marked, trail goes right. Follow this to Rainbow (3), 3.5 miles.

From McHugh Creek, the trail climbs high above Turnagain Arm, emerging from a cottonwood forest to a panoramic view. Here the trail passes under high, rocky, rotten cliffs. Be sure no one is on the cliffs above, watch for natural rock falls, and take care not to dislodge rocks because people may be below. Cliff scrambling here is dangerous.

Beyond the cliffs the trail enters pleasant woods. About 1½ miles from McHugh Creek, where a major creek drainage is on the right, the trail forks; take the upper fork.

From here the trail again climbs, then descends in switchbacks, crossing gravel Rainbow Valley road and continuing downhill to the Seward Highway. About 150 feet east of Rainbow Creek, the trail leaves the Seward Highway. It climbs a gentle grade and continues about 2 miles to (4) "Windy Corner" (repeater tower access). From "Windy Corner" a short, well-worn foot trail leads down to the Seward Highway.

From Potter to Rainbow this is a very good family trail, which can be traversed in short or long segments. Beyond Rainbow there has been less trail maintenance, as the trail has not been serviced in conjunction with overall trail renovation. In several sections southeast of "Windy Corner" the trail is obscured by natural land and rock slides. However, with cautious traverse technique, one can find the trail beyond the slide. Historically and in the future the trail will extend as far south as Girdwood.

There is seldom enough snow on this trail for skiing, but because of this the trail often provides good winter hiking. South from McHugh, where Turnagain Arm is visible bore tides may be seen, depending on the tide cycle, approximately 1¾ to 2 hours after the Anchorage listed low tide. (See Anchorage daily newspapers for tide times.)

Westbound and shorter trip directions:

(2) McHugh Creek access, mile 111.9, Seward Highway. To hike to Potter (3½ miles) take the left fork in the Picnic Site to the upper parking lot. The trail is marked, going from the upper end of the parking area.

(3) Rainbow Valley access, mile 108.5, Seward Highway. Park south of the highway. The trail to McHugh Creek (4 miles) begins east of Rainbow Creek at the east end of the guard rail.

(4) "Windy Corner," repeater tower access, mile 106.7, Seward Highway. Park north of the highway, just east of the repeater tower. Follow a well-worn trail uphill, bearing right onto a small ridge. Follow this ridge to the obvious old trail above (2 miles to Rainbow).

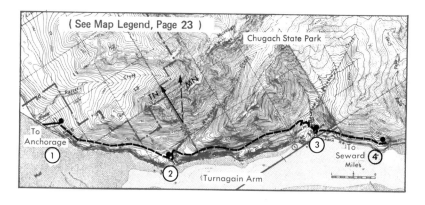

(See Map Legend, Page 23)

Chugach State Park

To Anchorage

To Seward

Miles

Turnagain Arm

Top: left, spruce grouse, May; right, parka squirrel cleaning up. Below: left, red fox, September; right, porcupine, September (Photos by Nancy Simmerman)

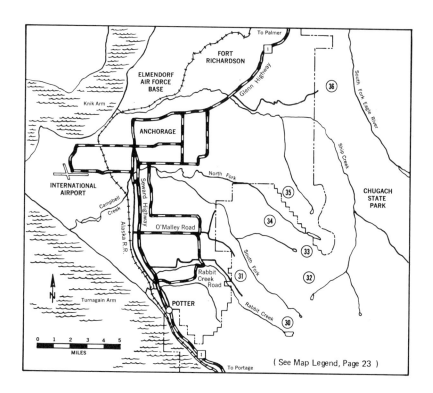

ANCHORAGE AREA

30 Rabbit Lake

Round trip 11 miles
Hiking time 5 hours
High point 3082 feet
Elevation gain 1280 feet
Best June—October
USGS maps Anchorage A7, A8
Chugach State Park

Blue-black waters below 2000-foot walls of the dramatic Suicide Peaks. The most accessible alpine lake in the Anchorage vicinity and a scenic delight. An excellent trip for children. Tempting camping.

From Sears in Anchorage, at Northern Lights Boulevard and the Seward Highway, drive south on Seward Highway about 7 miles to DeArmoun Road on the left. Drive east on DeArmoun about 4 miles to its intersection with Hillside Drive. Continue straight across Hillside Drive onto what is known as Upper DeArmoun Road. Beyond the intersection the road is not maintained and deteriorates considerably, but the condition varies from season to season.

Bear right on Upper DeArmoun Road, heading upvalley. Follow the main road to the Chugach State Park boundary (about 3½ miles). Ordinary two-wheel-drive cars should probably park here, though as of 1978 the continuing road is open to motorized vehicles for another 2½ miles and can be driven by some cars when the road is dry.

From the end of the old road it is about 2½ miles to Rabbit Lake. Now on foot, if not before, parallel a muddy jeep trail across the tundra to the lake. This track is an ugly and unnecessary scar marring a lovely valley; it stands as another monument to man's irresponsible use of technology. Now that the area is part of Chugach State Park use of vehicles beyond the end of the established road is prohibited. Report license numbers of offending vehicles to the Park office.

The lake lies at the base of the Suicide Peaks (5005 and 5065 feet), linked by the high saddle of Windy Gap. When there is no wind, camping here is delightful; however, have warm clothing, winds here can be fierce. No campfires are permitted. Swimmers have been known to try the lake. While not technical climbs, neither are the Suicides easy hikes. Several easier side-trips beckon the hiker, however.

One is to climb onto the ridge to the northeast. Just beyond the suggested parking point this ridge drops to a broad pass at 3500 feet. Climb 600 feet to this pass, and visit the small tarn nestled below the 1500-foot northwest flank of "Ptarmigan" Peak.

A second inviting side-trip is to climb the ridge which divides Rabbit Creek valley from McHugh Creek valley. From the lake, at 3082 feet, it is an easy climb to the first high point, 3810 feet, and from there a delightful ridge walk along the heights to whatever destination is chosen. It is about 3 miles to 4301-foot McHugh Peak from

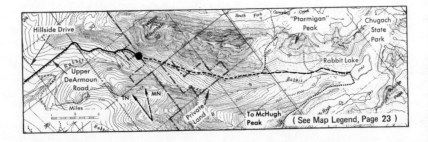

(See Map Legend, Page 23)

Moss campion or moss pink, July, 1½ times life size (Photo by Nancy Simmerman)

Rabbit Lake. Hikers can descend the ridge straight down to the floor of Rabbit Creek valley and return directly to the car. There is no water on the ridge. Do not attempt to follow McHugh Creek to the Seward Highway because of difficult bushwhacking in the last 2 miles.

When Chugach State Park is developed access is likely to change, as may the facilities and designated use of the area. At present it remains primitive, and the area beyond the end of the established road is reserved for foot travel.

31 Flattop

Round trip 4 miles
Hiking time 3-4½ hours
High point 3550 feet
Elevation gain 1350 feet
Best June—October
USGS map Anchorage A8
Chugach State Park, Anchorage Watershed

The "classic" afternoon hike near Anchorage. Because of long-time easy access, Flattop is probably the most frequently climbed peak in Alaska. The view from the top extends from McKinley in the northwest to Redoubt in the southwest. Though parts of the climb are steep, over loose rock, and without definite trail, it is not difficult. Small children and novices may have problems, however. Boots with good traction are desirable. On the shortest and longest nights of the year the Mountaineering Club of Alaska annually holds overnight outings on the summit, despite the lack of water. Flattop is a good winter climb for those properly equipped. Avalanches have killed people here on the north and southwest slopes. Do not slide down snow-filled gullies. See "Avalanches," p. 17, and check with Chugach State Park staff about current conditions before making a winter climb.

From Sears in Anchorage, at Northern Lights Boulevard and Seward Highway, drive south on Seward Highway about 3 miles to O'Malley Road. Turn left and drive about 4 miles to the intersection with Hillside Drive. Turn right on Hillside Drive and drive 1 mile to Upper Huffman (marked). Turn left and go straight for ¾ mile to a fork in the road. Take the right fork, Toilsome Hill Drive. This road switchbacks uphill for about 2 miles to the Glen Alps entrance to Chugach State Park. Park in the lot here (road beyond is private and signed against parking).

Many routes are possible, but the following is recommended. From the parking lot, follow the lower of 2 trails ½ mile to an avalanche-fire danger sign near a powerline. From here take the right-hand road of two which head south, paralleling the power- line. Follow this road about 50 feet and turn right on a rough road which leads toward Flattop. Keep left on this road through scrub hemlock to a large open area beyond the trees. Cross this and turn left onto an obvious trail traversing the slope more or less paralleling the ridge. This leads to a gully from the low saddle at 2500 feet which separates Flattop from the long low mound at the beginning of the ridge. The snow in this gully avalanches in winter. The trail crosses the gully and here is the northwest rock ridge, to the left of the gully on the west slope. A worn trail can be found up this ridge. In spring and early summer parts of the route are covered by snow.

It is unfortunate that operators of four-wheel-drive vehicles do not stay on existing trails. The ridge leading to Flattop is badly scarred by a network of wheel tracks,

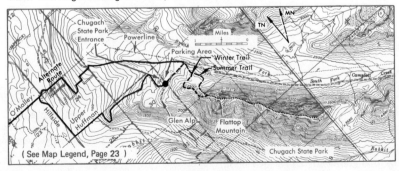

(See Map Legend, Page 23)

Kenai Peninsula and Turnagain Arm from Flattop, August (Photo by Gayle and Helen Nienhueser)

long-lasting proof that the tundra is indeed fragile.

From Flattop the hiker can follow the ridge 3 miles to its high point at 4500 feet. The ridge is exposed in some places, but the experienced hiker will encounter no real difficulty. He can return to the parking area by descending the steep northeast slope to the powerline road.

Loose rock on the upper reaches of Flattop constitutes a serious potential hazard, and people have been injured here by falling rocks. Never roll rocks down or allow your children to do so—there may be people below, and even a small rock can become a lethal weapon. Take care to avoid dislodging loose rocks, and if one is accidentally dislodged immediately yell "Rock!" at the top of your voice, and continue yelling until the rock is at rest.

Return to the parking area from the summit of Flattop offers a choice of obvious trails in summer. Stay on a trail, to avoid contributing to the growing problem of erosion which has been brought on by heavy travel in this area.

32 The Ramp

Round trip 12 miles
Hiking time 8-10 hours
High point 5240 feet
Elevation gain 3040 feet
Best June—September
USGS maps Anchorage A7, A8
Chugach State Park, Anchorage Watershed

A delightful easy summer walk to "Ship Lake" pass between Ship Creek and Campbell Creek drainages. Good for children to the pass, and a nice winter ski or snowshoe tour. From the pass it indeed appears to be a walk up a ramp to the summit of this 5240-foot peak — a moderately-steep climb with a 1200-foot elevation gain in about ½ mile. Good views of the Chugach Mountains from the top. An alternate and easier summit is The Wedge (4660 feet), southwest of the pass.

The Ramp, July (Photo by Nancy Simmerman)

From Sears in Anchorage, at Northern Lights Boulevard and the Seward Highway, drive south on Seward Highway about 5 miles to O'Malley Road. Turn left and drive about 4 miles to the intersection with Hillside Drive. Turn right on Hillside Drive and drive 1 mile to Upper Huffman (marked). Turn left and go straight for ¾ mile to a fork in the road. Take the right fork, Toilsome Hill Drive. The road switchbacks uphill for about 2 miles to the Glen Alps entrance to Chugach State Park.

On foot follow the lower of 2 trails ½ mile to the avalanche-fire danger advisory sign near a powerline. Turn right on the powerline road and follow it past 13 powerline poles, for about 2 miles, to a point where an old jeep trail comes in from the left at right angles. Follow the trail downhill to South Fork Campbell Creek. Normally it is possible to cross the stream here on rocks, but, during periods of high water, it may be necessary to wade. Follow the trail as it climbs the hill above the stream and through the brush to the stream draining the valley. Cross it where convenient and wander on up the valley on the right (south) side of the stream for easy brush-free walking. After the stroll to the pass (admire the headwaters of Ship Creek beyond) follow the ridge to the north to the summit of The Ramp.

Walking in the valley is freedom itself. All brush has been left behind and firm dry tundra, laced with occasional springs, makes distances seem short. Look for wildflowers in season, parka squirrels, and sheep. Enjoy the summer smell of heather on a warm sunny day. There are numerous inviting tent sites in the area and water is never far away. Campfires are prohibited. Carry a stove. This area is presently open to snowmobiles in winter when the Division of Parks determines that snow cover is sufficient. There is a potential avalanche hazard on all slopes and a potential for slab avalanches in snow-filled gullies when the slopes are bare.

From the pass below The Ramp it is possible to descend steeply down the east side to "Ship Lake." Follow its outlet downstream, veer around the corner to the right, and follow the center fork of Ship Creek upstream to Indian Creek Pass. From the pass follow Indian Valley trail to Indian (see Trip 27). About 11 miles one way — 1 or 2 days.

Another possible 1-day trip is to hike the powerline road over Powerline Pass and down into Indian Valley, easy walking but often marred by encounters with trail vehicles. Snow remains in the pass into July, but after that there is good camping near the streams on the southeast side and side-trips are possible. The terminus for this trip differs from the beginning of Indian Valley trail (see map with Trip 27). This route has extremely high avalanche hazard in winter. (See "Avalanches," page 17.)

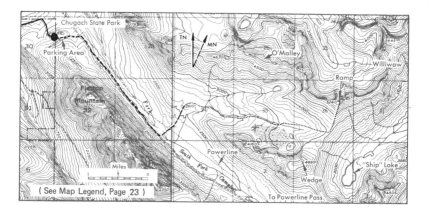

ANCHORAGE AREA

33 Williwaw Lakes

Round trip 12 miles; alternate 14 miles
Hiking time 8-11 hours
High point 3700 feet
Elevation gain 1600 feet
Best June—early October;
  winter: November—April
USGS maps Anchorage A7, A8
Chugach State Park, Anchorage Watershed

Alpine gems all different in size, color, shape and setting. Grassy meadows with scrub hemlock, tarns and rock ridges. A long 1-day trip but a lovely excursion into backcountry. The string of lakes at the base of Mt. Williwaw (5445 feet) offers inviting campsites for the backpacker. Campfires are prohibited, so bring a stove for overnight camping. There is no trail, but the route lies above timberline and with the aid of USGS topographical maps there is no problem finding the way. (To be safe bring a compass in the event of fog.) This would be a good overnight backpacking trip for families with older children, if the children are experienced hikers. There are blueberries, cranberries, and crowberries in season and a wide variety of alpine flowers.

From Sears in Anchorage, at Northern Lights Boulevard and the Seward Highway, drive south on Seward Highway about 5 miles to O'Malley Road. Turn left and drive about 4 miles to the intersection with Hillside Drive. Turn right on Hillside Drive and drive 1 mile to Upper Huffman (marked). Turn left and go straight for ¾ mile to a road fork. Turn right on Toilsome Hill Drive which switchbacks uphill for about 2 miles to the Glen Alps entrance to Chugach State Park.

On foot follow the lower of 2 trails ½ mile to the avalanche advisory sign near a powerline. Turn right for about 300 yards on the powerline road, then left on a trail leading downhill to the South Fork of Campbell Creek. Cross the stream on rocks; if the water is high, wading may be necessary. Climb the steep slope above the stream to the east, weaving through brush, to the pass at 3250 feet (point 3278 is on the left). Cross the sloping plateau beyond the pass, heading northeast to a second pass at 3700 feet. Tiny Deep Lake is tucked away to the right.

A reported alternate route to the plateau is to follow a trail north from the bridge as shown on the map. In a little over a mile, shortly after crossing a little creek, the trail goes over a knoll. At that point, leave the trail and bear right cross-country up to the plateau.

From the plateau descend a steep scree gully to Black Lake. Sturdy hiking boots are needed here. Pass the lake and continue the descent, now down a slightly more

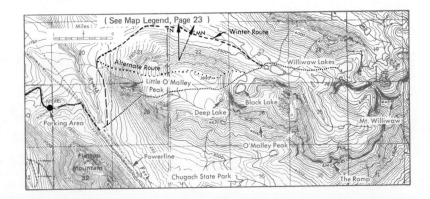

102

Moose calf, August (Photo by Nancy Simmerman)

gradual and tundra-covered rocky slope. Once on the valley floor (2600 feet) head upvalley, passing a group of lakes and gradually crossing over to the left side of the valley at any convenient point. Pass above the second group of lakes at the base of a ridge of Mt. Williwaw and climb about 300 feet to the final lake in a cirque below Williwaw (at 3300 feet). If the weather is good plan to linger here enjoying the solitude and magnificent alpine scenery.

On the return trip the steep scree gully can be avoided by climbing instead a steep tundra slope to the right of the gully. Near the top cut back to the left and the pass.

A 2-day circular trip could be made from the final lake by crossing the low ridge (3700 feet) above it to the northeast and dropping down into the valley of North Fork Campbell Creek. This valley can be followed down to the access to Knoya (see Trip 35). Map-reading skills are essential to find the way out.

In winter be aware of avalanche danger. (See "Avalanches," page 17.) The alternate route makes a good winter ski trip into the valley of the Middle Fork of Campbell Creek. Do not go up on the bench. In winter the brush is no problem; simply skirt the ridge and head upvalley as shown on the map. The area is closed to snowmachines west of the line between Flattop and "Little O'Malley."

34 Wolverine Peak

Round trip 10½ miles
Hiking time 6-9 hours
High point 4455 feet
Elevation gain 3380 feet
Best June—September;
    winter: November—April
USGS maps Anchorage A7, A8
Chugach State Park, Anchorage Watershed

Wolverine, the broad triangular mountain on the skyline east of Anchorage, is an excellent 1-day trip, offering views of Anchorage, Cook Inlet, the Alaska Range, and glimpses of the lake-dotted wild country behind the peak. A good winter mountaineering trip on skis or snowshoes, too. An old homesteader's road, now closed to vehicles, makes a fine trail to timberline for summer hiking and winter skiing. Parka squirrels,

Wolverine Peak from Anchorage, October (Photo by Nancy Simmerman)

spruce grouse, occasionally moose, and on rare occasions wolverine can be seen. Blueberries and cranberries in season.

From Sears in Anchorage, at Northern Lights Boulevard and Seward Highway, drive south on Seward Highway about 5 miles to O'Malley Road. Turn left and drive about 4 miles to the intersection with Hillside Drive. Turn left and immediately right again on Upper O'Malley Road. Follow this about ¼ mile to Schuss Drive, the second road to the left. (This is the first left turn after Hideaway Trail and a long row of mailboxes on the right.) Turn left and continue, bearing right and uphill at major intersections. In about a mile there is the Prospect Heights entrance to Chugach State Park and a parking area. Park here (elevation 1075 feet).

On foot follow the trail (old road) which leaves the parking area and heads east. Where the trail meets a powerline, turn left and continue on the main trail to the South Fork of Campbell Creek. Cross here on the bridge and follow the trail around a sharp switchback and uphill past a trail (old road) turning sharply right. (In winter this right fork leads to a fine ski trip into the Middle Fork of Campbell Creek.) Continue to the second trail (old road) to the right after the creek, about 1.1 miles past the creek and 2.3 miles from the parking lot. Follow this trail as it angles off uphill, starting at an elevation of about 1350 feet. The distance from here to the peak is about 3 miles. The trail deteriorates to a narrow path through brush, difficult to follow at times, but worthwhile. It finally becomes a moose trail through blueberry bushes, then vanishes, but at this point the hiker is above brushline. He should note well where he emerges from the brush in order to find the trail on his return. The route is marked with flags.

After the trail vanishes, go up toward the ridge on the right, watching for a moose trail and opening through scrub hemlock. This is the last hurdle; now the going is clear up the ridge to the peak, though from here the peak itself is not obvious.

There is no water on the route. The climb to the end of brush is a pleasant evening trip with a view of McKinley from that point.

Climbers may want to tackle the peak in winter, though some avalanche hazard may exist. (See "Avalanches," page 17.) The upper slopes are likely to be windpacked or windswept; the last part of the climb is on foot and crampons may be necessary.

A network of about 20 miles of ski trails now leaves from the parking area and is connected to the other 3 hillside entrances. The old road to its end and the side-trail to Middle Fork are popular tours; a leaflet showing other routes is available from the Chugach Park office at 2601 Commercial Drive and sometimes at the trailhead.

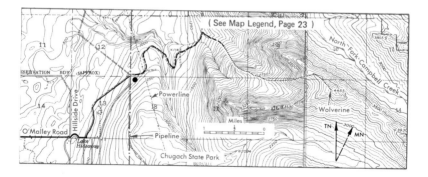

ANCHORAGE AREA

35 Knoya — Tikishla

Knoya round trip 13 miles
Hiking time 9-11 hours
High point 4600 feet
Elevation gain 3525 feet
Best late June—September
USGS maps Anchorage A7, A8

Tikishla round trip 15 miles
Hiking time 11-14 hours
High point 5150 feet
Elevation gain 4075 feet
Best late June—September
USGS maps Anchorage A7, A8
Chugach State Park, Anchorage Watershed

A choice of climbs, both with the same access route. Lower, closer, and easier, Knoya is reached by a long steep climb up its south slope. Tikishla, more interesting, is reached via a 2-mile long ridge. Both peaks offer fine views of Anchorage, Cook Inlet, McKinley and the Alaska Range. Or hike up the valley of North Fork Campbell Creek to 60-acre "Long Lake" in a cirque above timberline at the end of the valley. All three trips involve climbing from road's end at 1450 feet over Near Point at 3050 feet and dropping into North Fork valley at 2200 feet. Do not attempt this route in winter due to avalanche hazard. (See "Avalanches," page 17.)

From Sears in Anchorage at Northern Lights Boulevard and Seward Highway drive south on Seward Highway about 5 miles to O'Malley Road. Turn left and drive about 4 miles to the intersection with Hillside Drive. Turn left and immediately right again on Upper O'Malley Road. Follow this about ¼ mile to Schuss Drive, the second road to the left. (This is the first left turn after Hideaway Trail and a long row of mailboxes on the right.) Turn left and continue, bearing right and uphill at major intersections. In about a mile there is the Prospect Heights entrance to Chugach State Park and a parking area. Park here (elevation 1075 feet).

On foot follow the trail (old road) which leaves the parking area and heads east. Where the trail meets a powerline, turn left and continue on the main trail to the South Fork of Campbell Creek. Cross here on a bridge and follow the trail to its end, 2.7 miles from the car. From the main trail's end a trail heads to the right (southeast) back up the valley. Follow this through alder until the growth above thins to cottonwood trees and light brush. Leave the trail here and head for the ridge crest to the north and a large spruce tree, a nearly brush-free route. Above brushline choose between

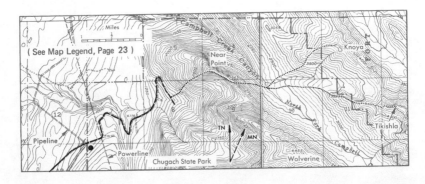

Tikishla and North Fork Campbell Creek, September (Photo by Gayle and Helen Nienhueser)

climbing over Near Point (easily identified by a survey tripod on its top) for easy walking and an extra 300 feet of elevation gain, or contouring along the sidehill below Near Point to the second notch in the ridge beyond at 2750 feet, the lowest of three notches. From the notch, eye the objective.

The route up Knoya (2 miles from the notch) lies east and slightly north, a steep but not difficult climb up the west ridge or the south slope with an elevation gain of 2400 feet from the valley. The route up Tikishla (3 miles) lies farther east and slightly south, offering an inviting ridge to its summit with an elevation gain of 2950 feet from the valley. The trip is often done in 2 days. In this case, camp at the stream, the only water on the trip. No firewood available. A traverse from Knoya to Tikishla is possible.

Those who prefer hiking can descend from the notch to the valley and explore its brush-free length to "Long Lake" at its head, about 5 miles away. An excellent 2-day circle trip would be to continue southeast, past "Long Lake," into the valley of Williwaw Lakes (Trip 33).

36 Rendezvous Peak

Round trip 3½ miles
Hiking time 3-5 hours
High point 4050 feet
Elevation gain 1500 feet
Best anytime
USGS maps Anchorage A7, B7
Chugach State Park, Anchorage Watershed,
Ft. Richardson Military Reservation

A good first mountain for children, a pleasant and easy trip for adults—with spectacular views of Mt. McKinley, Mt. Foraker, Cook Inlet, Turnagain and Knik Arms, Mt. Susitna, Anchorage, Ship Creek Valley, and Eagle River Valley and the peaks beyond it. In winter the trip to the pass is fun on cross-country skis even for the novice.

From 6th Ave. and Gambell St. in Anchorage drive northeast on the Glenn Highway about 6½ miles to Arctic Valley Road. This is a military road, and in winter chains or studs are required. Wind up this road about 7 miles. At the first fork, near timberline, take the right; at the second fork go left to the civilian ski area and parking lot.

From the parking lot, at about 2550 feet elevation, walk northeast up the valley, following wheel tracks and keeping to the right of the stream. After a short distance the track goes uphill to the right. Leave it, cross a small gully, and continue up the main valley to the pass. There is water only about halfway up the valley.

The pass itself (3468 feet) has lovely views, but those from the top of Rendezvous (4050) to the right (southeast) are even better. This part of the hike is steeper but short and worthwhile, leading to a craggy summit at the top. From the top there are good ridge walks back above the ski area and above the valley of the South Fork of Eagle River, but carry water. Hikers can choose their own descent route from the summit. The tundra-covered slopes are very inviting for rolling or sliding on your seat during descent for those young in years or at heart. In winter the snowpack in gullies and on north and northwest slopes may avalanche, so stay on the windblown ridge. (See "Avalanches," page 17.)

Since the access is on military ground, and subject to military control, there are infrequent times when restrictions are placed on its use or it is closed to civilians entirely. Generally no problems are encountered. Arctic Valley Ski Area is on public land leased from the state. The Ski Area buildings and equipment are private property. Please respect it and report any vandalism. The entire area is part of the Anchorage watershed.

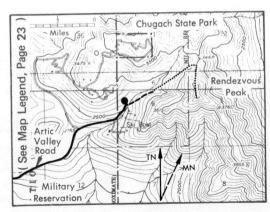

Sliding down the heather, September (Photo by Nancy Simmerman)

Rendezvous Peak, his first summit (Photo by Nancy Simmerman)

109

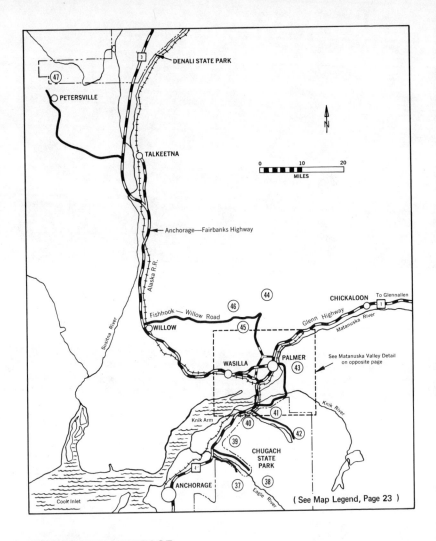

NORTH OF ANCHORAGE

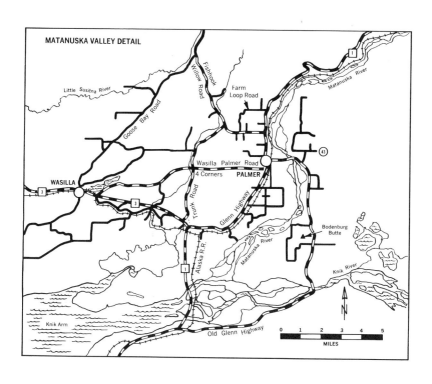

MATANUSKA VALLEY DETAIL

Little Susitna River

Willow Road

Fishhook

Farm Loop Road

Matanuska River

Goose Bay Road

Wasilla Palmer Road

4 Corners

PALMER

WASILLA

Trunk Road

Glenn Highway

Alaska R.R.

Matanuska River

Bodenburg Butte

Knik River

Knik Arm

Old Glenn Highway

0 1 2 3 4 5
MILES

N

Talkeetna Mountains at Hicks Creek, April (Photo by Nancy Simmerman)

37 Eagle Lake

Round trip 12 miles
Hiking time 8-10 hours
High point 2600 feet
Elevation gain 650 feet
Best June—early October
USGS maps Anchorage A7, B7
Chugach State Park

Because of current land ownership status and pending State purchase of access to Chugach State Park, hikers should **not** go up this valley until these matters are settled. Under no circumstances is the road from Throg's Neck Bridge up the valley to be driven or hiked. Even the hiking route described below is complicated by nearby houses and bush-whacking in the first part. It also involves several short stretches of private land. For details on possible revision in the access route, phone the Chugach State Park at 279-3413.

A lovely alpine glacier-fed lake, with a nearby clear-water companion. A pretty valley walk to get there, and beyond, a wilderness of rugged mountain peaks. A good winter ski or snowshoe tour.

From 6th Ave. and Gambell St. in Anchorage drive northeast on the Glenn Highway about 11½ miles to Hiland Road. Take the turnoff to the right just before the overpass, then immediately turn right again onto Hiland Road. Follow this for 3½ miles to the end of state maintenance. Take the right-hand fork, and after another 1½ miles take another right fork, staying on Hiland Road. After 0.4 mile go straight on Johnny Drive instead of following Hiland Road downhill to the left; avoid the driveway on the right. Follow Johnny Drive about ½ mile to its end and park away from houses, being careful not to block the road; it is a dedicated public road and dead ends at the Park boundary.

Avoid the private property at the road's end by heading straight into the brush from the end of the road, then angle uphill for a few hundred yards to an old road. Turn left on this and follow it about a mile to its end. From the end of the road, follow game trails through light brush paralleling the west bank of the creek. Head for low ridges on the valley floor. Their crests provide easy walking, and the brush thins out farther up the valley. Some boulder-hopping is necessary shortly before Eagle Lake.

From Eagle Lake (2600 feet) hikes and climbs abound. One is to follow the southwest edge of Eagle Lake about ½ mile, skirting boulders. Then turn right and climb over a low ridge (2750 feet) to the clear waters of Symphony Lake (2645 feet). The best campsite is here (no firewood). Watch for moose, black bear, Dall sheep, and mountain goat. From Symphony Lake the hiker can continue about 1½ miles south to two tarns (3400 and 3565 feet), situated in cirques and wreathed by alpine

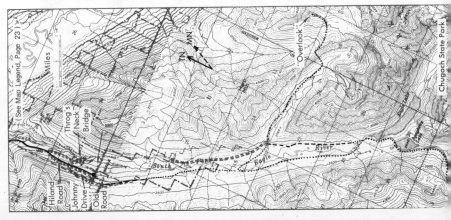

Pond enroute to Eagle Lake, June (Photo by Nancy Simmerman)

flowers. The ridge between these tarns leads to a high plateau (4500 feet) overlooking North Fork Ship Creek.

Challenging peaks for the experienced mountaineer include Cantata (6410 feet), Calliope (6810 feet), and Eagle Peak (6955 feet).

A side-trip for another day is Eagle River Overlook. Follow the road directions, then continue on foot upvalley about 2 miles. To the east, across South Fork, is a large valley, at right angles to South Fork valley. Cross South Fork and climb up into this side valley through brush, staying on the left (north) side of the main stream, following game trails. After about 2½ miles climb the steep grassy slope to the left (north) to a pass at 3850 feet. From here, stroll to points 5065 and 5130 ("Overlook"), both of which provide spectacular views of Eagle River Valley and the mountain wilderness beyond. From road's end to "Overlook" is about 6 miles one way.

38 Dew Mound

Round trip 7 miles
Hiking time 3-6 hours
High point 947 feet
Elevation gain 400 feet
Best May—October; winter: December—March
USGS maps Anchorage A6, A7
Chugach State Park

A pretty walk through woods over a well-defined trail, with magnificent mountain scenery all around. A good family hike in early spring. The route lies along the Girdwood to Eagle River part of the historic mail trail between Seward and the Interior (see Trip 25). A fine winter ski or snowshoe trip.

From 6th Ave. and Gambell St. in Anchorage take the Glenn Highway northeast about 13 miles to the exit for Eagle River business district. Turn right at the exit, onto the road coming across the overpass, and right in 0.1 mile in front of Eagle River School onto Eagle River Road. Continue about 10½ miles to the end of state maintenance. At the turnaround, go straight, following signs for Paradise Haven Lodge. Park at the lodge and ask permission of the owner to continue on foot.

Follow the road past the Lodge for several hundred yards to an old jeep road on the right marked with a "trail" sign. Follow this trail about a mile to the beginning of the Crow Pass Trail. There are several forks, but the trail is well marked with signs and arrows. The Crow Pass Trail, which turns left off the old jeep road, is prominently marked. Beyond the sign the trail is closed to motorized vehicles. In about a mile the trail parallels Eagle River briefly. Just after leaving the river there are traces of the old mail trail cut out of the hillside; boulders cover the right bank below the trail. Beyond this is old, rocky glacial moraine, dotted with scrub birch and spruce. The cliffs of Dew Mound are visible to the left. Continue through the rocky area, through a wooded patch, and up and down a little hill. At the foot of this little hill bear left, leaving the trail, and head for Dew Mound. This brings the hiker to the more gradual slope of Dew Mound, to the right of the cliffs.

The climb offers nice views back down the valley and of the wild, beautiful country

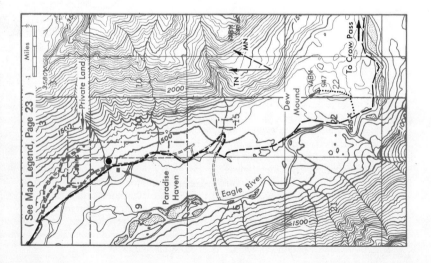

114

up the valley. The top is covered by scrub birch and spruce, but grassy spots offering nice vistas can be found.

When descending take care to avoid the cliffs by returning via the ascent route. Head south toward the river, skirting the hillock to the right, until running into the trail. Another 20 minutes' walk farther east along the trail brings the hiker to the river again. Those desiring a longer hike can continue along the newly cleared trail toward Crow Pass (see Trip 25). Another 2 miles brings the hiker to a view of lovely Heritage Falls on the south side of Eagle River. Campsites are available along the river. Watch for black bear and falling dead trees in the burned area.

This trail makes a fine cross-country ski trip in winter when there is enough snow. The last 2 miles of the road may be icy in spots, but the Lodge operators try to keep it open.

Eagle River, Dew Mound trail, May (Photo by Gayle and Helen Nienhueser)

39 Round Top and Black Tail Rocks

Little Peters access:
Round Top, round trip 8 miles
Black Tail, round trip 10 miles
Hiking time 7-9 hours
High point, Round Top 4755 feet
Elevation gain, Round Top 3755 feet

Meadow Creek access:
Round Top, round trip 8 miles
Black Tail, round trip 6 miles
Hiking time 6-8 hours
High point, Round Top 4755 feet
Elevation gain, Round Top 2655 feet
Best June—September
USGS map Anchorage B7
Chugach State Park

A panoramic view from Redoubt to McKinley rewards the hiker who makes the steep climb to Round Top's summit. Once there he will find all around him the Chugach Mountains, including Bold Peak in the Eklutna area, glimpses of the high Chugach behind it, and Eagle and Polar Bear Peaks in the Eagle River area. An easy short day outing takes the urban dweller into this mountain wonderland.

Two approaches are possible, via Meadow Creek and via Little Peters Creek. As of 1978, the Meadow Creek approach is easiest to find and offers the most elevation gain by car, but crosses some private land and involves climbing over Black Tail Rocks to reach Round Top. Though unmarked and therefore somewhat difficult to find at present, the approach via Little Peters Creek will eventually be the official Chugach Park entrance. (Call Park headquarters—279-3413— for current access information.)

Meadow Creek access: From 6th Ave. and Gambell St. in Anchorage, follow the Glenn Highway 13.6 miles to the Eagle River exit. Turn right at the exit, right onto the road coming across the overpass, and left in 0.1 mile onto the old Glenn Highway. Follow this 0.7 mile to Eagle River Loop Road; turn right. In 1.1 miles, where the Loop Road bears right, turn left onto Skyline Drive. This is a rough road but dry by early May and can be driven by most cars. Follow it 3.4 miles to the entrance to Meadow Creek

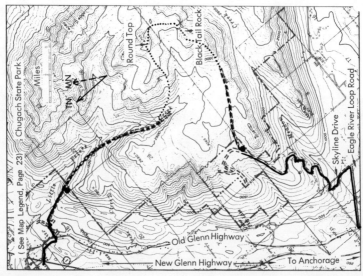

Ridge on Round Top, September (Photo by Gayle and Helen Nienhueser)

and a sign reading "The Wallace Bros. Mountain and Company." Park here (elevation 2100 feet).

On foot, follow the trail (old jeep road) which starts just beyond the entrance. It leads uphill to a broad plateau (3000-3300 feet). Follow the south edge of the plateau for ¾ mile to the east and the beginning of the west ridge of Black Tail Rocks. Climb this ridge ¾ mile to the summit (4446 feet). From the summit it is a relatively easy traverse along the ridge to Round Top (4755 feet) one mile to the north.

Little Peters Creek access: Follow the Glenn Highway about 20 miles to the exit sign for Birchwood Loop Road North. Turn right and in 0.4 mile turn right again onto the old Glenn Highway. In 0.2 mile turn left, the second left turn after Chugiak Chapel, shortly before a large gravel pit. Note the mileage when turning. Take the first left. Turn right 0.25 mile from the highway, then take the first left and follow it about a mile to the Chugach State Park boundary. The continuing road up the valley of Little Peters Creek has been blocked; park here off the road (elevation 1000 feet) or about ¼ mile before the barrier at a Y in the road.

From the barrier, hike up the trail (old road) about 2 miles. Locally this area is known as Ptarmigan Valley for the small ski area which once existed here. Follow a tracked-vehicle trail which turns left off the road shortly before its end and heads uphill. This climbs above the brush before petering out entirely. From there climb the tundra-covered slope to the right to a point on Round Top's west ridge. Follow the rocky ridge to a subsummit for a first view of Round Top, then on to the broad, lichen-covered top (4755 feet).

From Round Top ambitious hikers can follow the ridge to the southeast to Vista Peak (5070 feet). South and slightly west of Round Top is Black Tail Rocks, which can be reached by following Round Top's southeast ridge, then veering south and west.

There is no water available on the route. In early September there are blueberries.

Both Round Top and Black Tail Rocks can be climbed in winter; take care to use ridge approaches to both and avoid gullies because of avalanche hazard. Crampons will probably be necessary for the final steep parts which may be windpacked. The area is open to snowmachines when snow cover is sufficient; it is closed to all other off-road-vehicle use and the closure is strictly enforced.

40 Thunderbird Falls

Round trip 2 miles
Hiking time 1 hour
High point 400 feet
Elevation gain 300 feet
Best May—October
USGS map Anchorage B7
Chugach State Park

A lovely walk for families with small children — with picnic tables by a stream and a pretty waterfall at the end. This is one that can be done early in the year, though there is still snow by the falls well into May. The woods are dominated by birch, the forest floor laced with wild roses and fern. This is a good place to teach the children to recognize and stay away from devil's club, a prickly large-leafed shrub, up to 6 feet high, which can be found along the trail.

From 6th Ave. and Gambell St. in Anchorage drive northeast on the Glenn Highway about 25 miles to the sign for Thunderbird Falls. Turn right onto the old highway. In 0.4 mile, just before Eklutna River, there is a parking lot on the right. From here an excellent and well-maintained trail leads 1 mile to the falls and picnic area. The trail is dusty during dry weather and slick during wet weather but poses no problem. Near the end of the trail, just as you begin to hear the sound of the falls, the trail forks. Both forks go steeply downhill to the same place, but the right-hand one provides the more gradual descent to the stream.

As the falls cannot be seen from the picnic area, they are an extra dividend when hikers find them. A trail leads upstream about 100 yards to the falls, hidden in the back of a narrow canyon where the sun reaches only a few hours a day.

Take care in allowing children to explore the cliffs because of danger of falling. At least one fatality has occurred in this manner.

This long-time favorite trail is losing some of its charm because the land through which it passes is being subdivided. Houses will be visible from the trail, though probably not from the falls. A 25-foot-wide easement has been reserved for the trail.

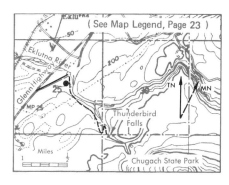

Thunderbird Falls, May (Photo by Gayle and Helen Nienhueser)

Trail to Thunderbird Falls, May (Photo by Gayle and Helen Nienhueser)

119

41 East Twin Pass

Round trip 8 miles
Hiking time 7-8 hours
High point 5050 feet
Elevation gain 4150 feet
Best July—September
USGS map Anchorage B6
Chugach State Park

Continual views of Twin Peaks while climbing to the pass and a panorama of the Matanuska Valley from the top. An excellent walk even on a gray day when clouds come and go around the peaks. Eklutna Lake is an aqua beauty below. Chances of seeing Dall sheep are good. An abandoned road helps get above brush and alders to open country.

From 6th Ave. and Gambell St. in Anchorage drive northeast on the Glenn Highway about 25½ miles to the exit for Eklutna Lake. Interchange construction is planned for 1978; when completed, turn right onto the exit ramp, right onto the crossroad, and immediately left onto the frontage road which will lead to the lake. About 10 miles up this road, at the lake, there is a small parking area. From this point continue on the main road an additional 0.4 mile, and turn left on a side-road just across a stream. In about 100 yards take the next left fork and go about ⅛ mile to a circular turnaround. Park here (elevation about 900 feet).

About 50 feet beyond the turnaround is a sign saying "Twin Peaks Trail 3.5 miles." Walk past this about 100 yards to a fork. Both forks go to the same place—the choice is between the right-hand road which switchbacks northwest higher up, or the left fork which shortly becomes a trail. This is the shorter but steeper route; in about ½ mile the trail rejoins the road. Follow the road about 2 miles from the parking area to its end at brushline. There are views of the lake behind and of Twin Peaks to the north as you climb.

The road's end at about 2700 feet (2½ to 3 hours round trip) may be destination enough; a lovely stream rushes down through a small canyon in the alpine bowl and camping or picnicking is tempting. Water is available at the stream, a short distance below the road through high grass. (No water along the way until this point.)

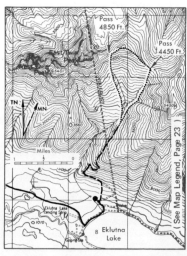

120   *Grizzly bear, July (Nancy Simmerman)*

East Twin Pass, looking into the Matanuska Valley, November (Photo by Gary V. Hansen)

To continue to the pass, head diagonally down to the stream through the high grass. There is a trail of sorts from the end of the road to the first draw coming down from the peak to the northeast, and down this draw to the stream. However, it is easy to lose; should this happen, simply descend to the stream and head for the low 4450-foot pass to the northeast. The high grass is soon left behind. Good views from this pass, but for the best Matanuska Valley vistas follow the ridge top northwest to the 5050-foot knob. To descend continue west to the pass at 4850 feet and down the steep south slope from there, staying on the west side of the stream below the pass for the easiest route.

The usual approach to climb East Twin is from the end of the road to the 4850-foot pass and up the east ridge of East Twin. The climb requires experience and mountaineering equipment.

The Eklutna Lake area is open for snowmobile use. See Trip 42 regarding conflicts with native claims.

42 Bold Peak Valley

Round trip 6 miles (currently 16 miles)
Hiking time 4-5 hours (currently 9-10 hours)
High point 3400 feet
Elevation gain 2500 feet
Best late June—early October
USGS map Anchorage B6
Chugach State Park

A hike up an old road from Eklutna Lake to Bold Peak valley at timberline. An unsurpassed September outing when Bold Peak is topped with white, the valley carpeted in red, the hillsides below sheathed in gold, and the lake a lovely aqua, but beautiful any time and in some ways more pleasant prior to hunting season, which begins in mid-August. In addition to lovely vistas there are ground squirrels, moose, sheep, goats, magpies, beautiful wildflowers, and, in season, blueberries and high-bush cranberries.

From 6th Ave. and Gambell St. in Anchorage drive northeast on the Glenn Highway about 25½ miles to a road on the right marked by a large sign for Eklutna Lake. About 10 miles up this road, at the lake, there is a small parking area. At the time of printing, the road is closed to motor vehicles about ¾ mile beyond this point because of wash-outs.

From the parking area continue on the main road around the lake about 5½ miles to a large stream which goes under the road through four large culverts. Cross it, go 150 yards, and turn sharply left onto the old road. If driving, park here. The trail begins 50 yards north of the junction and is marked by a trail sign (elevation 900 feet).

Head uphill on foot. The trail climbs steeply through timber to brushline at about 2500 feet. Stay on the main trail, ignoring turnoffs. Nice views of the lake are often available on the way up. Once above brushline the trail continues into the valley for nearly another mile to an elevation of about 3400 feet. The stream shown on the USGS map is partially underground. It is on the surface at the head of the valley by the gravel moraine, then goes underground, and does not reappear until it is parallel to and about ¼ mile beneath the end of the trail. There are good campsites or picnic spots along the stream.

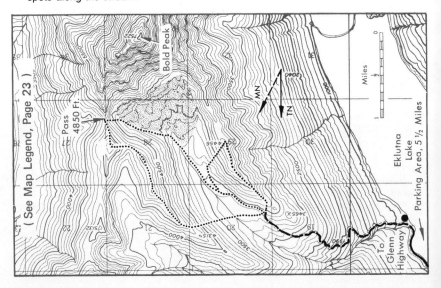

Bold Peak from Eklutna Lake, September (Photo by Nancy Simmerman)

From the end of the trail a variety of side-trips is possible. A good one is a climb up onto the ridge to the right (south). Once on top walk the heights to point 4456 feet for magnificent views of Bold Peak (7522 feet), Eklutna Lake and Glacier, and all the mountains in the area. One can return to the road's end by descending to the valley floor and walking the length of the valley back to the road.

Another good trip is to walk the valley nearly to its end and climb to Hunter Creek Pass to the east at 4850 feet, just below point 5281 feet. From the top of point 5281 there are good views of the relatively-inaccessible Hunter Creek valley and the still largely untouched mountain wilderness rising beyond it. This goal can also be reached by climbing the left-hand or north ridge back at the end of the trail and ridge-walking to the southeast to point 5281. Bold Peak should only be attempted by experienced climbers. The Eklutna Lake Road is not kept open in winter past the beginning of the lake. This area is open for snowmobile use when the Division of Parks determines that snow cover is sufficient.

Portions of this area have been selected by the native village of Eklutna under the Alaska Native Claims Settlement Act of 1971 (ANCSA).

At the request of the Mountaineering Club of Alaska, the Bureau of Land Management recommended reservation of easements for Bold Peak, East Twin, and Round Top trails. The reservation is not assured until the land is conveyed, but MCA expects the trails to be reserved. MCA's position is that public rights to these trails are not extinguished by ANCSA.

43 Lazy Mountain

Round trip 5 miles
Hiking time 5-6 hours
High point 3720 feet
Elevation gain 2900 feet
Best May—October
USGS map Anchorage C6

A pleasant but steep uphill hike with a craggy summit and glorious view at the top. The climb has been made by children as young as 4 years; they, of course, take a bit more time. The downhill part is especially good for running, jumping, and sliding. The Matanuska Valley, fertile farming center, spreads out below the peak. To the northeast the upper valley becomes pinched between the Chugach and Talkeetna Ranges. To the south the Knik and Matanuska Rivers join to flow into Knik Arm, and Pioneer Peak soars majestically above the Knik River. Bodenburg Butte shows clearly as a knoll to the west of the old Glenn Highway.

Follow the Glenn Highway northeast out of Anchorage 42 miles to the third turnoff for Palmer, West Arctic Street, easily identified by a Tesoro Station on the corner. Follow this road 2.3 miles (crossing the Matanuska River) to Clark Wolverine Road (marked). Turn left on this for 0.6 mile to a T-junction. Turn right on Huntly Road for 1 mile to the crest of the hill. Park.

To the left of the two continuing roads a trail heads north up the bank past powerline pole LM/6/19/3E. After about 100 yards, the trail turns sharply right. Stay on it and honor "No Trespassing" signs. It is an overgrown jeep track which soon becomes a trail, well-defined all the way to brushline. There is only one confusing fork; take the right. The lower portion of the trail winds through low brush and tall grass which may be wet with rain or heavy dew even on a clear dry day, so be prepared for damp feet and clothes. The path becomes quite steep and in spots sometimes very slick with mud. After the first of several false summits, where the growth gives way to low berry bushes, the going becomes gentler. From here on pick your own route up the tundra-covered slopes. The last 200 feet of the summit ridge are narrow and exposed; children will need help. There is no water anywhere on the route.

Wildflowers abound; new flowers introduce themselves with every hundred feet of elevation gained, culminating on the crest in minute lichens with brilliant pinhead-sized sporangia clinging to the rock.

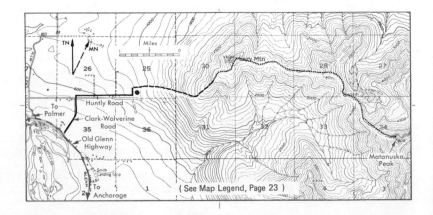

(See Map Legend, Page 23)

View of Matanuska Valley from Lazy Mountain (Photo by Pete Martin)

Energetic hikers may want to continue on to Matanuska Peak (6119 feet), the real mountain looming to the east. This is a long 12- to 14-hour hike round trip, but more than half the elevation is gained by the time you reach the summit of Lazy Mountain; much of what remains is a long ridge walk, culminating in rock-scrambling. At the end of the long ridge between Lazy Mountain and Matanuska Peak, head to the right up the northwest ridge of Matanuska Peak. From the top of this ridge approach the summit rock pile up a loose scree slope. Go right at the final rocks. A rope is not necessary if the route is carefully chosen. A flashlight is desirable except during the longest days. This elevation is not usually snow-free until July.

44 Reed Lakes

Round trip 6 or 8 miles
Hiking time 5-7 hours
High point 4250 feet
Elevation gain 1550 feet
Best July—September;
    winter: November—April
USGS map Anchorage D6

Granite spires, alpine lakes, and waterfalls, reminiscent of the high Sierra, on the edge of the vast wilderness of the Talkeetnas, a mountain world unlike any other near Anchorage. Watch for ptarmigan, marmots, ground squirrels, pikas, northern shrike, and eagles.

Drive the Glenn Highway about 35 miles to the junction with the Anchorage-Fairbanks Highway (Route 3). Turn left, and in 0.4 mile turn right on Trunk Road. Follow Trunk Road 8 miles to Fishhook-Willow Road. (See area map page 111.) Turn left and continue 11 miles to Little Susitna Roadhouse. Turn sharply left around the roadhouse and continue 1 mile to a fork. Turn right. (The main road continues to Hatcher Pass.) From here the road deteriorates but can be driven by most cars. Drive

Pool en route to Lower Reed Lake (Photo by Gayle and Helen Nienhueser)

2.5 miles to a fork, the second right after Archangel Creek. Turn right here on Snowbird Mine road. (The left fork goes to Fern Mine.) In 0.6 mile there is a wide area where most cars should park. The continuing road is very rough and high clearance is needed. Driving time from Anchorage is about 2 hours.

Hike down the road 1 mile to its end at a privately-owned house and ruins at abandoned Snowbird Mine Village at 2700 feet. Upper Reed Lake is 3 miles from here; Lower Reed Lake is 2 miles. The hanging valley of Glacier Creek, to the northwest, is a nice side-trip. Reed Creek valley is not obvious from the mine buildings; the creek comes down from the middle valley to the north. Look for waterfalls partway up it. Take the gravel road 200 feet past the wooden frame house and veer off it to the right, directly opposite the garage, on a narrow trail. Cross the first creek (Glacier) on a wooden aqueduct. About 300 feet through tall grass cross Reed Creek on large granite boulders beside a partially-submerged pipe. In years of high water this crossing can be difficult and wading necessary. Bushwhacking uphill along the left streambank is possible. After crossing the stream the trail is obvious through the grass, but the hiker should note where he crosses the stream and starts on the trail or he will miss the crossing on his descent. The trail climbs steeply up a hill, then contours left below the hilltop to an area covered by large granite boulders. Boulder-hopping is necessary here, making the trip difficult for inexperienced hikers, young children, older people, and dogs. After leaving the boulder field, follow sparkling Reed Creek through grassy meadows and past small crystal-clear pools which reflect the surrounding mountains. Good camping is available from here on, and hardy types have found these pools possible for swimming. No firewood, but plenty of water. Cross to the north side of the creek at these pools, and climb 200 feet to the aqua beauty that is Lower Reed Lake (elevation 3750 feet), staying high on the left above the stream. Many hikers will find this a good destination.

Upper Reed Lake is another mile. To the left, 300 feet above Lower Reed Lake, is a lovely waterfall cascading over slabs. To reach the upper lake skirt around the falls to the left over grassy meadows and rocks. An additional half-hour takes the hiker past a shallow lakelet to another vivid aqua lake (Upper Reed Lake), larger than the lower one, set in a cirque at the base of Lynx Peak (6536 feet). Granite spires and faces rise steep and high above talus and glaciers. These lakes are often still ice-covered in July. Good camping on mossy hummocks even here at 4250 feet.

The 4-mile trip from Hatcher Pass road to Snowbird Mine is a good winter ski or snowshoe tour over level or gently-sloping terrain. Take a shovel to dig out a place to park off the road. Snowmachines use the area to a limited extent.

This area has been proposed for inclusion in a state park or state recreation area.

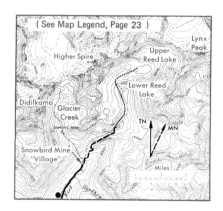

45 Hatcher Pass Ski Tour

One-way trip 14 miles
Skiing time 5-8 hours
High point 3886 feet
Elevation gain 950 feet
Best November—April
USGS maps Anchorage D7, D8

A beautiful winter ski tour through the Talkeetna Mountains on the unplowed Fishhook-Willow Road. A short 1½-mile climb with an elevation gain of about 950 feet places the skier at Hatcher Pass, and from there it is all downhill for about 12½ miles. Total elevation loss is about 2350 feet. Mountains rise on both sides of the road, garbed in winter finery. The major flaw in this rosy winter picture is the 2-hour drive between the two ends of the trail. The easiest way to handle this is to arrange to be picked up at the Willow end of the trail. The trip is more pleasant on a weekday because of weekend competition from snowmachines, particularly in January and February, due to racing activities.

Drive northeast out of Anchorage about 35 miles on the Glenn Highway to the Anchorage-Fairbanks Highway (Route 3). Turn left here and in about 0.4 mile turn right on Trunk Road. Follow Trunk Road 8 miles to Fishhook-Willow Road. (See area map, page 111, to clarify direction at intersections.) Turn left (north) on Fishhook-Willow Road and continue about 15 miles, passing through the scenic gorge of Little Susitna River, and climb above timberline. Two miles before reaching Independence Mine, the A-frames of the Hatcher Pass Corporation stand on a knoll on the right side of the road. Park near here in an area provided. During winter 1977-78 the road was plowed almost to the A-frames. The road is steep, narrow, and winding, and chains may be necessary.

From the parking area follow the unplowed road past the A-frames until the valley leading to Hatcher Pass comes into view. It may be possible to see the road switch-backing up the valley to the west. Follow this or a route of your own choosing up the valley to Hatcher Pass. The snow on this side of the pass is generally hardpacked by snowmachines. Then begin the downhill run to Willow Creek bridge through pleasant mountainous terrain. Snowmachine use on the west side of the pass is less extensive. Routefinding is no problem as the drainage pattern is definite and leads to the bridge. Note the old mine buildings high on the slopes to the right near Craigie Creek. From the Willow end the road is plowed 15 miles to Willow Creek bridge. This makes a good destination, though some may prefer to ski the remaining distance to Willow. It is

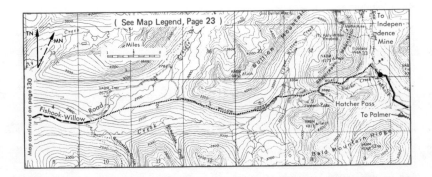

Route to Hatcher Pass, November (Photo by Nancy Simmerman)

possible to go from Willow to Anchorage by the Alaska Railroad on certain days. Check with them for current schedules.

An alternative 1-day trip is to ski in the Independence Mine bowl. The Independence Mine Lodge has reopened and offers meals, bar, and limited overnight accommodations. The Lodge is about a mile from the parking area described above; the road from the parking area to the Lodge is privately maintained and often requires four-wheel drive or chains.

The weather in the Hatcher Pass area often can be still and warm, but it is unpredictable; wind gusts are possible, creating ground blizzards on the clearest of days, and temperatures are generally colder than in Anchorage. In midwinter, daylight lasts only from 8:30 a.m. to 3 p.m. Take extra warm clothes and a flashlight with strong batteries. Avoid steep slopes during avalanche conditions. (See "Avalanches," page 17.)

To reach the Willow end of the trail from Independence, drive about 10 miles back toward Palmer. After leaving the mountains take the second road to the right, just beyond a road to Edgerton Park. This is the Wasilla-Fishhook Road and is marked "Wasilla 11." Follow this road to Wasilla. In Wasilla turn right (west) onto Alaska Route 3, Anchorage-Fairbanks Highway, to Willow. Turn right off Route 3 onto Fishhook-Willow Road at a sign for Hatcher Pass, and drive for 15 miles to the Willow Creek bridge. To reach Willow from Anchorage follow the Anchorage-Fairbanks Highway.

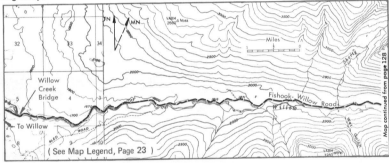

Willow ptarmigan in winter plumage (Photo by John Ireton)

Winter at Hatcher Pass (Photo by Nancy Simmerman)

46 Craigie Creek

Round trip 3 miles
Hiking time 1-3 hours
High point 4250 feet
Elevation gain 950 feet
Best July—early October
USGS map Anchorage D7

A beautiful summer drive over Hatcher Pass, culminating in a short walk to an alpine tarn rimmed by precipitous peaks and spires. Good for the whole family. An excellent departure point for hiking, exploring, and climbing deeper in the Talkeetna Mountains.

Drive the Glenn Highway about 35 miles to the junction with the Anchorage-Fairbanks Highway (Route 3). Turn left and in 0.4 mile turn right on Trunk Road. Follow Trunk Road 8 miles to Fishhook-Willow Road. (See area map, page 111.) Turn left on Fishhook-Willow Road and continue 11 miles to Little Susitna Roadhouse. Turn sharply left around the roadhouse and continue about 3½ miles to the turnoff to Independence Mine. Where that turnoff goes straight, turn left across a stream. Continue over Hatcher Pass approximately 6½ miles to a side-road turning right into the valley of Craigie Creek. The road over Hatcher Pass is narrow, steep, and winding, unsafe for campers and trailers. It is not open until mid-June and then may be wet, rough, and soft.

At the turn onto Craigie Creek road note, high on the mountains to the left, the mine shafts of Lucky Shot and War Baby Mines. Goldmining in the Craigie Creek area began prior to 1919 and continued at least through 1930. It gradually died out as inflation made it uneconomical, but a few mines in the area still show signs of small-scale activity. When the route was checked no areas were posted against trespassing; however, the route may cross private property. Should signs be posted, respect them. In any case, do not disturb buildings or equipment, do not remove rocks or other minerals, and ask permission to continue should buildings be occupied.

Craigie Creek road is rough and not maintained. The intersection with Fishhook-Willow Road may be impassable. If it is dry, cars with high clearance and good traction may be able to drive almost 3 miles. About 2.8 miles from the main road, look for a place to park. Take the first possibility (a spot on the right where the ruins of a cabin can be seen across the creek); the road becomes impassable beyond this.

From here (elevation 3300 feet) continue on foot, following the old road which climbs gently, passing old buildings and waterfalls. The road ends at Dogsled Pass (elevation 4250 feet), where there is a lovely blue-green tarn. The far side of the pass

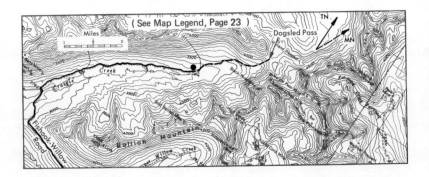

Beyond Dogsled Pass, Purches Creek headwaters (Photo by Gayle and Helen Nienhueser)

is covered by acres of granite boulders. Plan a picnic by the lake. No firewood.

Hikes and climbs abound. From the pass it is an easy walk up the west ridge to several high points. A rock scramble up the gully next to Black Prospect Mine shaft brings one to the ridge overlooking historic Independence Mine. From Dogsled Pass the hiker can head north to the Kashwitna River drainage, through an area of alpine lakes and peaks between 5000 and 6000 feet. Another possibility is to bear right across the flat area beyond Dogsled Pass, climb to a 5150-foot pass leading to the high valley containing Talkeetna Mine, drop into that valley, on into Fairangel Creek valley, and out to Fern Mine road (see Trip 44).

In winter the road over Hatcher Pass is closed beyond the Hatcher Pass Corporation A-frames.

47 Peters Hills

Round trip 4 to 14 miles
Allow 3 hours-2 days
High point 2840 or 3929 feet
Elevation gain 1000 to 2100 feet
Best July—September
USGS map Talkeetna C2
Denali State Park

A delightfully different hike for southcentral Alaska, dominated by Mt. McKinley ("Denali") looming 40 miles to the north. Marvelous campsites at small lakes dotting the hills; a good backpacking trip with children. While the view of "Denali" from point 2840, a 2-mile walk, is excellent, the view from Long Point (a 7-mile walk to 3929 feet) is straight up the Tokositna Glacier, unobstructed by the Dutch Hills, and breathtaking. The drive from Anchorage takes 4 to 5 hours. Look for blueberries in season, and watch for grizzlies. This is a particularly nice early-fall hike during the week, though swarming with hunters and all-terrain vehicles on weekends.

Take the Anchorage-Fairbanks Highway (Route 3) to mile 115, 16½ miles past the Talkeetna turnoff, and turn left on Petersville Road opposite Cache Creek Standard Station, marked by a sign for "Peters Creek 19."

Peters Hills are 31 miles away. The first 8 miles of this road were reconstructed in 1974 and the next 11 miles are fair to Forks Roadhouse and Peters Creek. Turn right at the roadhouse. The road deteriorates at this point. It is narrow and poorly maintained, but when the road is dry (usually by July), it is possible to drive it in cars with sufficient clearance. (Call the Department of Transportation for a road report.) Continue 11 miles past Forks Roadhouse to the mine at Petersville. Drive about 1 mile farther and look for a tracked-vehicle trail to the right. Park near here.

The trail leads a short distance through brush to open country. Here consult the USGS map and plot destination and route. It is an easy walk to point 2840, which is not visible from the end of the trail. Head for the obvious high point, and the route to the top will be evident. The lakes near point 2840 offer good camping, though no wood is available. Intrepid souls have been known to swim here.

If time permits, go farther. The small lake at about 3350 feet in Section 34 on the USGS map, the source of Cottonwood Creek, makes excellent camping with a superb view of "Denali" and its consorts. From there the trip to Long Point is a gently-rising 2-mile walk.

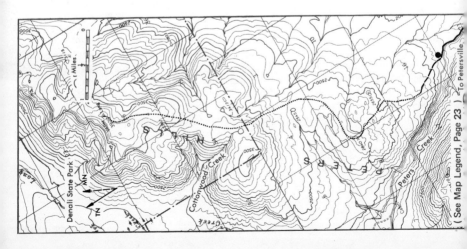

Mt. McKinley from Peters Hills, September (Photo by Nancy Simmerman)

Sydney Laurence painted his pictures of "Denali" from just below Long Point. A hotel has been proposed for a site north of the Peters Hills in the general vicinity of Ramsdyke Creek. The road would be extended to the hotel site. As of 1978, the Alaska Division of Parks is studying the feasibility of the project.

Golden birch (Photo by Nancy Simmerman)

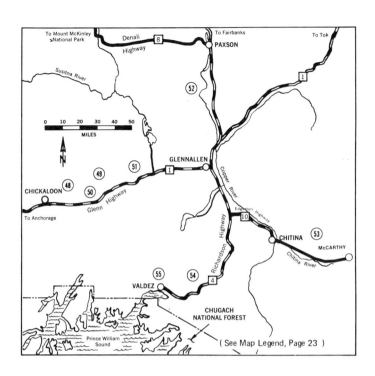

CHICKALOON TO VALDEZ

CHICKALOON TO VALDEZ

48 Hicks Creek — Chitna Pass

One-way trip 42 miles
Allow 4-5 days
High point 4700 feet
Elevation gain 2934 feet;
 total gain 3875 feet
Best late June—September
USGS maps Anchorage D2, D3, D4

An introduction to country which invites endless wandering. The Talkeetna Mountains: a true wilderness of peaks, valleys, tundra, and clear mountain streams, far from civilization, inhabited by moose, black bear, grizzly bear, sheep, wolves, and coyotes. A circular route is described, but many other trip possibilities exist, limited primarily by the backpacker's time and ability to carry enough food. Though lovely in early September, this country is then invaded by hunters; hikers may want to plan their trip earlier.

This is not a marked, maintained trail but rather a collection of swamp-buggy, horse, and game trails. It is not a trip for the novice, because help is far away. But experienced backpackers, in good condition and able to follow USGS topographical maps, will find this a delightful experience.

At mile 99.2 Glenn Highway, opposite powerline pole 7746, turn north onto a dirt road. Park here or on the south side of the road. Do not block the road. The beginning of the trail is known locally as either Pinochle Creek Trail or Hicks Creek Trail.

(See Map Legend, Page 23)

138

Crossing Boulder Creek, August (Photo by Nancy Simmerman)

On foot follow the road north. It quickly becomes a tracked-vehicle trail which climbs eventually from 1776 feet to a 3150-foot pass above timberline. The trail is deeply rutted and mucky in places, an example of what mechanized transportation does to wet tundra country. Additionally, the landscape is marred by litter, left behind by thoughtless hunters. But the total trip is worth this initial visual discomfort.

From the pass, the trail descends to Hicks Creek at 3000 feet. A nice side-trip is to head northwest, across the creek, toward a small lake about 5 miles away, at 5000 feet. There is good camping here (no firewood) and the peak above the lake, Monarch (7108 feet) is the highest in the area and an easy, though steep, climb.

The main trail continues to Hicks Lake where there is a good campsite at the south end. High country beckons. The vegetation is primarily dwarf birch, willows, and moss; watch for muskrats, ptarmigan, and parka squirrels. Beyond Hicks Lake the route is a bulldozer and swamp-buggy trail. It crosses a low 3300-foot pass, then follows a small stream down to Caribou Creek (2800 feet), about 4 miles from Hicks Lake.

Follow the trail up Caribou Creek on its south side, passing several good campsites. Look for agate, jasper, and other brightly-colored rocks. Just above the junction with Billy Creek, cliffs make it necessary to climb the bank and travel the bluff until the route is clear below. Do not cross Caribou Creek at any point. The trail shown on the north side on the USGS map is nonexistent.

Near Chitna Pass, August (Photo by Nancy Simmerman)

Above the junction of Chitna and Caribou Creeks, the trail follows the south bank of Chitna Creek a short distance, then drops to the creek (where there is a good campsite) and climbs the opposite bank. Chitna Creek is swift, but not deep nor difficult to cross.

Above Chitna Creek the trail blends with competing game trails. It does continue to Chitna Pass, though searching may be necessary. About 2½ miles from Caribou Creek, turn northwest, following a tributary of Chitna Creek toward Chitna Pass. At 3600 feet the terrain suddenly changes from brush to open tundra—delightful walking. Chitna Pass is 2½ miles away, at 4700 feet, a gradual climb on game trails to tempting camping and exploring country. Plenty of water, no firewood, easy climbing to peaks just under and over 6000 feet.

Just south of Chitna Pass the trail is well-defined. Follow it as it parallels a small creek. Where the small stream enters a canyon, about 2½ miles from the pass, the trail stays on the ridge northwest of the canyon. It does not cross into Boulder Creek drainage here as shown on the USGS map.

About 4 miles from Chitna Pass the trail reaches Boulder Creek. Here the well-defined path ends; most hikers have walked the stream bed, splashing back and forth across the braided channels. If the water is low, this is the easiest route along Boulder Creek. If the water is high, cross the stream once and stay on the northwest side. This side is easiest, and occasional stretches of trail can be found. It should be possible to stay on the southeast side, though some scrambling up bluffs may be necessary. The best camping along Boulder Creek is on the river bed.

About 7 miles down Boulder Creek, on its west side, and shortly before the entrance of East Boulder Creek, is a private cabin. From this point downstream, and out to Chickaloon, is a well-defined horse trail.

According to oldtimers, prospectors in the early 1900s traveled this trail from Knik (which could be reached by boat in summer) to Chickaloon, up Boulder Creek, over Chitna Pass, and along Caribou Creek to Alfred Creek. (See Trip 49). Their destinations were gold prospects and mines on Alfred and Albert Creeks. Trips 48 and 49 can be combined in several different ways as perusal of the USGS maps indicates. Caribou Creek is difficult to cross, however, particularly downstream from Trip 48.

Exiting via the Purinton (Puritan) Creek trail is the recommended route because it is a spectacular end to the trip. Leave Boulder Creek stream bed just before reaching the bluff of Anthracite Ridge, and find a trail on the east bank of the stream and at the base of Anthracite Ridge. This is the Purinton Creek trail, marked on USGS maps as Chickaloon-Knik-Nelchina trail. Follow this trail south and then east.

Coming around the end of a low ridge, suddenly a panoramic view of the rugged Chugach Mountains appears, across the Matanuska River to the south. The trail has some boggy places, but the rest is good walking. Little water is available, and few desirable campsites.

To reach Purinton Creek trail by road, drive to mile 89, Glenn Highway. About 100 feet east of Purinton Creek is a dirt road heading north. Follow this road north, then east. Park at a tracked-vehicle trail leaving from this road and ascending a very steep hill to the north.

This trip should be a good winter ski tour as a day trip from either end or as a several-day trip for experienced ski tourers and winter campers. The trail is likely to be packed by occasional snowmachines at the Purinton Creek end and may be used by tracked vehicles at the Pinochle Creek end.

49 Squaw Creek to Belanger Pass

One-way trip 25 miles
Allow 3 days
High point 4350 feet
Elevation gain 1650 feet
Best June—September
USGS maps Anchorage D1, D2

This trip demands sturdy hiking boots, good physical condition, backpacking experience and equipment, ability to read a topographical map, and a sense of humor. The reward is a marvelous 3-day wilderness experience in the Talkeetna Mountains. Usually this is isolated country but after caribou hunting season opens in mid-August, wear bright colors! Look for ptarmigan, parka squirrels, rabbits, porcupines, water ouzels, hawks, moose, caribou, black bear, grizzly, coyotes, wolves, and sheep. Certainly tracks and droppings will be plentiful and the coyote or wolf call may be heard. Blueberries and the gamut of Alaskan wildflowers in season; good fishing in Squaw Creek. This would be a glorious early-September trip when the mountains are clad in scarlet, but September is also hunting season.

The route follows the valleys of Squaw, Caribou, Alfred, and Pass Creeks, thence over Belanger Pass, in a circular trip around Syncline Mountain. Tracked-vehicle trails can be followed in places, but elsewhere hikers must search for game trails. Hiking time averages about 1 mile per hour in this terrain. In the early 1900s the Alfred Creek part of the route was traveled by prospectors coming from Knik Arm by way of Chitna Pass (see Trip 48). Gold was discovered on Alfred Creek in 1911, but prospectors were also going beyond Alfred to Albert and Crooked Creeks.

The trip can be taken in either direction, but starting at Squaw Creek is recommended.

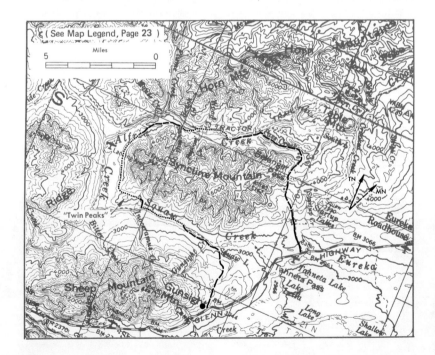

Campsite overlooking Caribou Creek, July (Photo by Gayle and Helen Nienhueser)

Park in the gravel pit at mile 117.6, Glenn Highway (opposite powerline pole No. 7151), elevation 3350 feet. A sign, "Squaw Creek trail," marks the beginning of the tracked-vehicle trail (locally known as Meekin's trail); follow it north over the toe (3600 feet) of Gunsight Mountain and down into the valley of Squaw Creek at 2700 feet, a distance of about 3 miles. In places this trail is very wet. Those who take more than 3 days will find beautiful camping in another mile in spruce woods just across Gunsight Creek. Soon the trail is swampy again, however, and in midsummer mosquitos are plentiful! As the trail nears Squaw Creek (about a mile beyond Gunsight Creek) it forks; the most-used fork appears to cross the stream, though actually it weaves back and forth, and there is no one clear trail. Cross the stream here (no problem normally—about a foot deep) and parallel the creek on the north side for about 2 miles, winding through brush until running into a well-defined tracked-vehicle trail going straight uphill. Follow it up and left (west) until it peters out again. Continue cross-country, heading for the pass between two bumps (locally known as "Twin Peaks") which separate Squaw Creek valley from Caribou Creek valley. From here to Alfred Creek there is no trail, but usually a game trail can be found through the brush. Stay high (about 3200 feet) while contouring around northern "Twin Peak" and begin looking for a campsite. Some streams on this east slope are underground in spots so listen for water. The only wood generally available is scrub willow. Total first-day distance about 9 miles.

The second day contour around Syncline Mountain into Alfred Creek valley, following game trails. Note on the USGS map the plateau near the base of the northwest side of Syncline Mountain, overlooking Alfred Creek. Follow the stream that flows between this plateau and Syncline Mountain. Here pick up a good foot trail, apparently man-made years ago. This gradually leads to the elevation of the plateau. Where the trail veers right, leave it, climb a small bank, and rest on the plateau while enjoying the view of a new valley.

Head northeast across the plateau, then follow a game trail down to Sawmill Creek and follow the creek to its junction with Alfred Creek (elevation 2900 feet). To the left, down Alfred Creek, are an old sawmill and cabins; to the right, up Alfred Creek, are another cabin and an old mine. Do not disturb either buildings or equipment as they are private property. Paralleling Alfred Creek is another tracked-vehicle trail. It is deceptive, however, as it weaves back and forth across the stream. Ignoring the trail, ford the stream at the first wide place upstream from the cabins. (Do not follow the south bank as cliffs make this impossible.) This is a potentially dangerous stream as it is at least knee-deep and very swift.

On the north side follow the tracked-vehicle trail where possible and bushwhack or follow gravel bars where there is no trail. Once past the cliffs (about 2 miles downstream from Pass Creek) recross the stream where the trail does. This crossing is easier, and a good trail continues on the south side to Pass Creek. Hikers who camp at Pass Creek the second night will have an easy last day. Total second-day distance about 9 miles.

Pass Creek should be easy to find as an excellent trail leads up it. Look for a stream that comes from a broad pass. In early summer ice may cover the trail beginning so that it is not obvious.

From the junction of Pass and Alfred Creeks (elevation 3400 feet) to the Glenn Highway hiking time should be 4 to 5 hours (about 7 miles). Hikers who leave a car at the end of 2-mile Martin Road leading in from Glenn Highway will take less time. The climb to the pass (4350 feet) is gradual; as usual, expect wet feet as the trail zigzags across the small stream. The view of the Chugach during the descent from the pass is magnificent, a fitting climax to the trip (elevation loss about 1400 feet). Respect and circumvent private property encountered where the tracked-vehicle trail joins the road. The trip ends at mile 123.3 on the Glenn Highway, at the junction of Martin Road and the Glenn Highway, opposite Tahneta Inn. Ask permission to park cars at Tahneta Inn or at Gunsight Mountain Lodge, ¼ mile west.

Caribou, September (Photo by Nancy Simmerman)   145

Gunsight Mountain from the Glenn Highway, July (Photo by Gayle and Helen Nienhueser)

CHICKALOON TO VALDEZ

50 Gunsight Mountain in Winter

Round trip 4½ miles
Hiking time 8-10 hours
High point 6441 feet
Elevation gain 3141 feet
Best February—April
USGS map Anchorage D2

Gunsight Mountain is a peak about 70 miles west of Glennallen, named for the distinct notch between its two summits. An excellent winter climb for all, from the experienced mountaineer to the novice just trying winter climbing. Proper winter gear, good physical condition, and experienced companions are a must, however, for the beginning winter mountaineer. The climb is not difficult, and the far-ranging view of the Wrangell, Chugach, and Talkeetna Mountains is superb. Lucky hikers may glimpse a band of caribou. A summer climb of the peak is possible, of course, but would include some bushwhacking.

The best approach in summer is via Squaw Creek Trail described in Trip 49. This trail takes the hiker past the worst of the brush, and he can then choose his route to the summit.

For a winter climb, drive to mile 118.4 on the Glenn Highway, where a creek crosses the highway (at about 3300 feet). This is a dip between two hills, marked with a "40 mph" sign. To the south is a road leading to the White Alice System Radio Relay Site. Park in a pull-out provided just west of the dip.

Walk the short distance to the creek and don snowshoes or skis. Because of the climbing involved, snowshoes should be wrapped with cord to provide greater traction, and climbing skins should be used with skis. Head northwest up the gully of the creek, staying on the left side of the stream and gradually climbing the ridge above the stream, winding around some brush. Head toward the mountain, eventually veering southwest (left) toward the highest (southeast) summit of Gunsight (6441 feet).

This is the easier of the two summits. Most of the climb is gradual and poses no problem. The last few hundred feet are steeper; snowshoes or skis will have to be cached and the remaining distance covered on foot. The snow is likely to be hardpacked, and vibram soles are necessary for adequate traction. Crampons may not be necessary, but carrying them on a winter climb is always advisable.

The traverse of the notch and the ridge between the two summits requires technical skill, especially in winter. It is not excessively difficult, but does require rope, crampons, experience, and involves rappelling; it is not recommended for the beginner. It is possible to bypass the notch on the back (south) side and thus avoid the rappelling. The mountain can also be climbed via the northwest summit, starting from the creek. The ascent to this peak is not technically difficult either, though there is some exposure. For the experienced and equipped climber a circular trip involving an ascent of both peaks and a traverse of the connecting ridge is probably most enjoyable.

Winter clothing appropriate for arctic conditions is mandatory. Temperatures frequently reach 25° to 35° below zero, and wind can increase the chill factor still further. Double boots (such as Lowa boots) or the military-type Korean boots should be worn. Remember that Alaskan winter days are short; watch the time, take a flashlight, and keep its batteries warm.

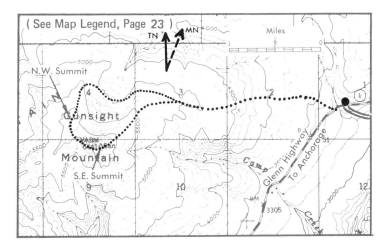

51 Slide Mountain

Round trip 6½ miles
Hiking time 6-8 hours
High point 3700 feet
Elevation gain 1300 feet
Best June—September
USGS maps Gulkana A6, Valdez D8

Slide Mountain, 46 miles west of Glennallen, is particularly fascinating for its geological history and its fossils. An excursion to the brushy summit provides views of the Wrangell, Chugach, and Talkeetna Mountains. Since it is nearly a 3-hour drive from Anchorage, hikers from that area may prefer to camp overnight at nearby Little Nelchina River Campground, mile 137.6, Glenn Highway (often crowded, however).

More than 80 million years ago, during the Mesozoic era, Slide Mountain and the surrounding area were buried under the sea. Sometime later the entire region was uplifted to form mountains and plains. But as a result of millennia under the sea, the mountain is rich in shell fossils, ancestors of today's clams and oysters. Other fossils, ammonites, and ancestors of today's octopus can also be found. The area has been picked over by fossil hunters, but new slides occasionally bring more specimens to the surface.

At mile 141.1, Glenn Highway, park near the Alaska State Highway Department maintenance station. Respect the NO TRESPASSING sign and walk around the station through the light brush to the back of the gravel pad. A tracked-vehicle trail starts near the middle of the back of the pad as a grassy road.

Follow the trail about ¼ mile; take the middle route when a three-way fork is reached, and follow it through the bog in an easterly direction. When another track takes off to the north (left), follow it up the mountain. At timberline, 2.5 miles from the starting point, the trail stops. From here it is easy walking for another ¾ mile, through light brush, to the top of the bluff, following animal trails.

From the blufftop enjoy the panoramic view of Tazlina Lake in the southeast to Gunsight Mountain in the southwest. Note the interesting strata of stream-rounded rocks in the buff-colored escarpment to the right (noted as survey point Horn on the USGS map). As the lake names indicate, fossils have been found at various places on this mountain, though they are not always easy to find. The brush covering the top of this mountain is likely to discourage the hiker from continuing to the actual high point, 4000 feet.

There are other approaches to the mountain and to reported fossil beds in various escarpments. One such area can be reached by hiking up the tracked-vehicle trail from the

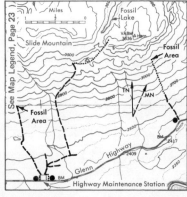

Lupine, June (Photo by Nancy Simmerman)

northwest corner of the State Highway Department gravel pad for about 2 miles (4 miles round trip). Another area is reached from a point near mile 144, leaving the highway on the north side. Plan to bushwhack and ask at the Nelchina Cafe for more specific directions.

As is common in the Interior, most of the flat areas are wet, either bogs or moist tundra. Waterproof footgear is desirable. Due to moisture, there is very little to encourage camping at the base of the mountain. Several good spots can be found from the first-described trail leading up the mountain. Drinking water is hard to find, although one pleasant stream flows near the trail about halfway up the mountain. The trail up the mountain is an ugly scar recently slashed through the forest, but it is walkable and, hopefully, it will soon revegetate.

Stream-washed outcropping near summit of Slide Mountain, June (Photo by Nancy Simmerman)

CHICKALOON TO VALDEZ

One-way trip 80 miles
Allow 4-7 days
Gradient 16 feet per mile overall
Best late June—early September
USGS maps Gulkana B3, B4, C4, D4

52 Gulkana River

A challenging and exciting kayak, float, or canoe trip through rolling, forested hill country with abundant wildlife and occasional views of the impressive Wrangell Mountains. Portions of the first part of the trip, from Paxson to Sourdough, are difficult; the rapids in this section should be run only in a rubber raft or by experienced canoeists or kayakers. The second part of the trip, from Sourdough to Gulkana, is suitable for canoeists with some experience in rapids. Splash covers for canoes and kayaks are necessary for the Paxson-Sourdough section and recommended for the Sourdough-Gulkana section. If planning a trip on the first section in June, call Paxson Lodge to be sure the ice on Paxson Lake is out; the lake generally breaks up in late June.

Drive to a new state campground on Paxson Lake, mile 175 on the Richardson Highway (10½ miles south of Paxson). The kayak route begins in Paxson Lake. A 1.6-mile gravel side road leads from the Richardson Highway down to Paxson Lake and the campground. Use the 500-foot boardwalk to cross the marshy area between the campground and the lake. There is no boat ramp here; there is one at the campground at mile 179.5, Richardson Highway, 4 miles north. The first part of the trip, from Paxson to Sourdough, is about 45 miles long.

Paddle south on Paxson Lake to the lake's outlet. The first 3 miles of the river are rocky, shallow rapids; the river drops 25 feet per mile in this stretch (Class III canoeing, difficult). After the junction with Middle Fork the river is pleasant and relatively calm for 15 miles (Class II, medium).

About 18 miles from Paxson Lake a canyon begins and with it about ¼ mile of rapids, the most difficult water described in this book (Class IV, very difficult). The river is deep but has rocks; the gradient is 50 feet per mile. Boats can be portaged for this short distance along the left bank on a trail. Boaters will be able to see and hear

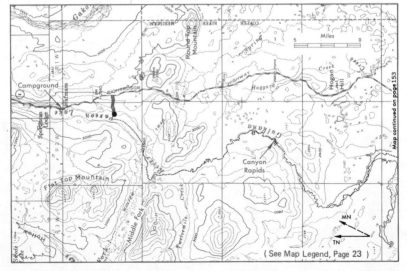

(See Map Legend, Page 23)

Gulkana River below canyon rapids, August (Photo by John Ireton)

Canyon rapids, August (Photo by John Ireton)

the beginning of the canyon rapids in plenty of time to get to shore. The trail begins just upstream of the first white water. The next 8 miles of the river are rough but not excessively difficult. The remainder of the river to Sourdough is Class II.

From Sourdough to Gulkana, 35 miles, the river closely parallels the highway. The rating varies from Class II to Class III and the gradient from 15 to 25 feet per mile. The major part of all this water is pleasant, with riffles and pools, interesting but not difficult. The last 8 miles to Gulkana are brisk Class III rapids—lots of fun. The Sourdough entrance or exit is at Sourdough Creek Campground, mile 147 on the Richardson Highway. The exit at Gulkana is at mile 127 on the Richardson Highway, where the highway crosses the river.

Caution is the word for those traveling from Paxson Lake to Sourdough. The entirety of the 45 miles is far from the road system. The frigid Alaskan waters make capsizing particularly undesirable and dangerous. Lifejackets and wet suits or warm clothing should be worn and at least two boats should make the trip, always maintaining sufficient distance between them to allow complete freedom of route. Boaters should beach their craft before the rapids and hike downstream for a good look before entering the rapids.

Campsites abound along the route with plenty of wood and water available. Watch for moose, beaver, muskrat, otter, caribou, grizzly bear, red fox, king salmon, rainbow trout, grayling and white fish from Paxson to Sourdough.

Classifications used are those designated by the Bureau of Land Management in its folder, **Alaska River Trails, Southern Region.** Information on the Gulkana River is included. Contact BLM at 4700 E. 72nd Street, Anchorage, Alaska 99507 (344-9661), for a copy. Some whitewater paddlers feel that BLM has in some cases overrated the difficulty of Alaska Rivers. Nevertheless, the Gulkana River canyon rapids are not suitable for inexperienced paddlers in open canoes.

The Gulkana River from Paxson Lake to Sourdough has been proposed for National Wild River status, and at the time of this writing legislation to accomplish this is pending in Congress. The southern portion, from Sourdough Creek to Gulkana, passes through lands selected by the Gulkana Village Corporation under the Alaska Native Claims Settlement Act of 1971.

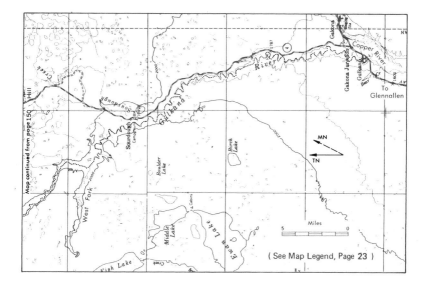

(See Map Legend, Page 23)

CHICKALOON TO VALDEZ

53 McCarthy to Kennicott

Round trip 12 miles
Hiking time 1 day
High point 2000 feet
Elevation gain 600 feet
Best June—September
USGS map McCarthy B6
Wrangell-St. Elias National Park

Remnants of Alaska's colorful history amid some of the state's most breathtaking scenery: Explore a ghost town, visit the ruins of the famed Kennicott copper mine, ride a cable tram, hobnob with a glacier.

From Richardson Highway mile 82.6 take the Edgerton Highway to Chitina, 33 miles. Chitina has the last gas and groceries; none are available at McCarthy or in between. Continue through Chitina to the bridge across the Copper River. The 63-mile rough gravel road ahead of you follows the bed of the old Copper River and Northwestern Railroad which, from 1911 to 1938, ran between Cordova and Kennicott. Allow 4 hours minimum on the road; railroad spikes scattered along the road threaten tires and the rough surface mandates a speed of 30 mph or less. Essentially a single lane with wide spots for passing, the road is not recommended for large RVs, trailers or low-slung automobiles. Check with the Department of Transportation and in Chitina for current road conditions. The road terminates at the Kennicott River.

The two bridges across the Kennicott River, just before McCarthy, are out indefinitely. In 1981, the first was still safe for foot traffic, but may not withstand the next high water. If this occurs, a cable tram will be put into operation. Park your car a safe distance from the river. To cross the second channel of the Kennicott River, use the existing tram. Pull steadily without jerking, otherwise the rope may jump off the pulley. McCarthy residents assume no liability for the safety of the tram system—inspect it before you cross.

After crossing the Kennicott River, follow the gravel road east, up a small rise to a major intersection. The well-traveled left fork goes to Kennicott mine, 6 miles away. The right fork takes you into the town of McCarthy. (An alternative access to McCarthy is to charter a plane in the Glennallen-Gulkana area or take the Tuesday mail plane, arrangements made through Ellis Air Service, P.O. Box 106, Glennallen AK 99588, phone: 907/822-3368.)

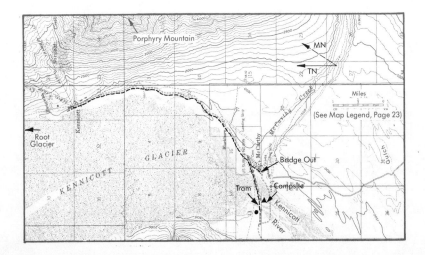

Kennicott Mine ruins (Photo by Nancy Simmerman)

After copper was discovered in the area in 1898 and mining begun in 1906, McCarthy sprang up—a mining boom town with a population of about 125 people. The mines and railroad shut down in 1938, and Chitina, McCarthy and Kennicott became near ghost towns. Establishment of a road on the old railroad bed from Chitina to the Kennicott River has brought new life to McCarthy, but most residents like McCarthy's isolation and lack of automobile access and hope that the Kennicott River bridges will not be rebuilt. McCarthy provides an excellent jumping-off point to the southern portions of the Wrangell-St. Elias National Park which surrounds the town. A state-maintained air strip lies northeast of the town. The bridge across McCarthy Creek and the road south of town were washed away in autumn 1980.

Be sure to check out McCarthy Lodge, open for business on an irregular basis for meals and beverages. Originally built in the early 1900s, the relic-filled structure has had frequent additions, but retains its 1920s flavor. Browse among the old photos on display in the lobby. The old McCarthy General Store, built in 1911 and now a National Historic Building, was leaning precariously until it was restored and renovated into a hostel, with family-style meals and basic but comfortable sleeping rooms. (Sleeping bags necessary.)

If you wish to camp in the McCarthy area, residents ask that you do so near the Kennicott River, downstream from the tram. Excellent drinking water is at Clear Creek which you will cross walking to the townsite. Be careful not to contaminate the stream; McCarthy residents use this creek for their drinking water. Please remember that *all* structures and land in the townsite are privately owned—do not scrounge for relics or use old lumber for firewood.

Several day hikes and overnight trips are possible from McCarthy. Ask locally for suggestions. The most popular trip is a day or two spent wandering among the buildings at Kennicott. Walk the easy 6-mile road to Kennicott or ask around McCarthy—sometimes a resident offers rides and/or tours of the Kennicott area. The mill and company town ruins sit along side the Kennicott and Root Glaciers. Additional buildings, a strenuous 5 miles away, sit high above on Bonanza Peak. In its heyday, Kennicott was a fully-equipped company town, complete with school, movie theater, general store, hospital and assay lab. Today the main activity is at Kennicott Glacier Lodge, a restored millworker residence, which has rooms and meals by reservation. There is no campground. (Call Trident radio phone patch service, 907/345-1140, or write: McCarthy via Glennallen, AK 99588). Once again, remember that all structures are privately owned.

To reach Kennicott from McCarthy, walk northeast on the only well-traveled gravel road. Since this road, too, lies on the old railroad bed, the grade is gentle.

54 Worthington Glacier Overlook

Round trip 1½ miles
Hiking time 1½-3 hours
High point 3000 feet
Elevation gain 800 feet
Best late June—September
USGS map Valdez A5

A trail for the more adventurous hiker who has good hiking boots (with vibram soles) to aid him. The whole Thompson Pass area, 25 miles north of Valdez on the Richardson Highway, offers good, easy hiking as the terrain is all above timberline, and the heather and smooth rocks are inviting. This particular trail, which follows the ridges of lateral moraines alongside Worthington Glacier, leads to impressive glacier views, but the last part is exposed, with steep drops to the glacier below.

From milepost 28.7 on the Richardson Highway follow the spur road west to Worthington Glacier State Public Campground. (This is suitable only for camper trucks and picnickers, as there are no tent sites or water. One could, however, camp in the meadows nearby.) Park in the lower parking lot, marked by a sign and outhouses. A prominent gray knob can be seen up the glacier near the icefalls, about a mile away. This knob is a good destination. The first half of the trail is not exposed, but beyond that caution is necessary.

Walk west up a low gravel ridge. Follow this low ridge a few hundred feet up to the main moraine and take a trail to the left which leads through a small willow patch to the higher moraine ridge above. Scramble up the side of the moraine and follow this ridge upward. The trail along the moraine top soon reaches an abrupt end at a cliff. Just before this, a trail leads left through small willows to a lush green meadow of heather, moss, and wildflowers. To get back to the glacier's edge go up the meadow, pick up the trail again in an alder patch, and climb onto another moraine. While wandering up through the meadow, note the cracks in the thin soil cover on the right where the rock

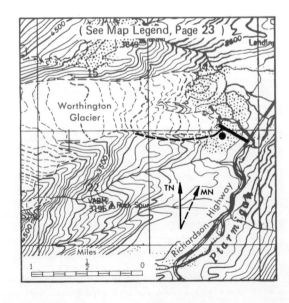

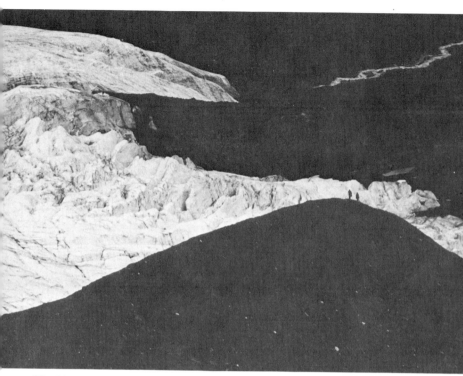

Worthington Glacier from trail, August (Photo by Nancy Simmerman)

masses are in the process of breaking off to fall to the glacier below. The meadow makes a good picnic spot. Then continue up the next moraine to the gray knob above. The view of the upper glacier from this knob makes the effort worthwhile. The hiker finds himself looking down from the trail into deep crevasses in the glacier, while standing on firm ground with soft green meadows nearby. Note the blue of the glacial ice. Don't let cloudy or misty weather cancel the hike. The blue of the ice is more intense on gray days, and the sculpturing of the ice is impressive at any time. In addition, the trail gives a hint of the thrill of mountaineering.

There is neither drinking water nor wood along the trail. The best camping in this vicinity is at Blueberry Lake Campground, mile 23 on the Richardson Highway.

"Smith Mill," Mineral Creek, August (Photo by Nancy Simmerman)

CHICKALOON TO VALDEZ

55 Mineral Creek

Round trip 2 miles
Hiking time 1-2 hours
High point 650 feet
Elevation gain 100 feet
Best June—September
USGS map Valdez A7

For the visitor to Valdez who is looking for a leg-stretcher, Mineral Creek is the answer. An old roadbed leads up this narrow, lush green canyon, and no matter what the weather, the area is beautiful. It is perhaps even more dramatic on a cloudy day when low clouds swirl through the canyon, changing its moods from moment to moment. Sometime this may be a route to the tempting alpine country surrounding Valdez, but at present the trail ends in brush, and travel beyond the trail's end is difficult and unpleasant.

If driving, follow the Richardson Highway past old Valdez to new Valdez, rebuilt in this location after the 1964 earthquake demolished the old townsite. The tourist may also reach Valdez via the Alaska State passenger and auto ferry **M. V. Bartlett,** sailing from Whittier several times weekly. See Trip 21 for directions to Whittier from Portage, mile 80 on the Seward Highway, or from Anchorage.

As the Richardson Highway reaches new Valdez, it becomes Egan Drive. Turn right (north) on Hazelet Avenue, and drive 10 blocks to Hanagita Street. Turn left, go one block, turn right, and at the next intersection, bear right onto Mineral Creek Drive, a gravel road. Go straight at the top of the first rise, not up to the water tanks. Drive this scenic but poorly maintained road 5.5 miles. Beyond this point, the road is unsuitable for vehicles. Park in this vicinity, off the traveled area.

Continue straight ahead, on foot, on the old roadbed. The trail parallels Mineral Creek, but remains well above the rushing water. A short distance before Brevier Creek, the trail turns right to historic Smith Mill, on the bank of Mineral Creek, a rock-crushing mill which once processed the gold-bearing rock obtained from the numerous mines in the area.

Hikers can continue to the banks of Brevier Creek, where most will want to stop. To reach high country from here involves considerable bushwhacking. The entire Valdez area is brushy without relief, except on recently-glaciated slopes where brush has not yet had time to develop. Hiking trails in this vicinity are needed to appreciate fully this immensely scenic area.

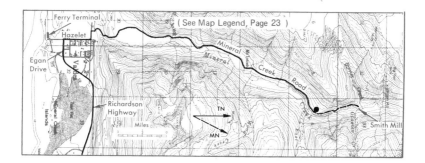

TIME OF YEAR

Summer trips are listed by the month the route generally is snowfree enough for use. Conditions vary greatly from year to year.

APRIL
1 Homer Beach Walk
10 Race Point
26 Bird Ridge
28 Table Rock
29 Old Johnson Trail

MAY
2 Swan Lake and Swanson River Canoe Routes (late May)
3 Seven Lakes Trail
4 Hidden Creek Trail
4, 7 Kenai River Trail
5 Skilak Lake Lookout Trail
7 Kenai River Canoe Trip
8 Lower Russian Lake
12 Ptarmigan Lake
14 Caribou Creek Cabin
14 Trout Lake, Juneau Lake, Swan Lake (cabins)
16 Hope Point
17 Gull Rock
19 Byron Glacier View
23 Winner Creek Gorge (late May)
27 Indian Valley
28 Table Rock and beyond
36 Rendezvous Peak
38 Dew Mound
40 Thunderbird Falls
43 Lazy Mountain

JUNE
6 Fuller Lakes
8 Russian Lakes-Cooper Lake Trail
9 Crescent Lake-Carter Lake
11 Lost Lake (late June)
13 Johnson Pass
14 Resurrection Pass Trail System
22 Alyeska Glacier View
23 Winner Creek Trail
25 Crow Pass (mid-June)
25 Crow Pass to Eagle River
27 Indian to Ship Creek
30 Rabbit Lake
31 Flattop
32 The Ramp
33 Williwaw Lakes
34 Wolverine Peak
35 Knoya-Tikishla Peaks
35 North Fork Campbell Creek
37 Eagle Lake
37 Eagle River Overlook
39 Round Top
42 Bold Peak Valley

48 Hicks Creek-Chitna Pass
49 Squaw Creek to Belanger Pass
51 Slide Mountain
52 Gulkana River
53 McCarthy—Kennicott
54 Worthington Glacier Overlook (late June)
55 Mineral Creek

JULY
15 Palmer Creek
18 Turnagain Pass
21 Portage Pass
41 East Twin Pass
43 Matanuska Peak
44 Reed Lakes
46 Craigie Creek
47 Peters Hills
50 Gunsight Mountain in summer

WINTER
1 Homer Beach Walk
2 Swan Lake and Swanson River Canoe Trails (lakes-ski touring)
3 Seven Lakes Trail
4 Hidden Creek Trail
4, 7 Kenai River Trail
5 Skilak Lake Lookout Trail
6 Fuller Lakes
8 Russian Lakes-Cooper Lake Trail
9 Carter Lake-Crescent Lake
11 Lost Lake
13 Johnson Pass from Moose Pass
14 Resurrection Pass Trail System, Hope to Cooper Landing
18 Turnagain Pass Ski Tour
19 Byron Glacier View
20 Portage Lake Ski Tour
23 Alyeska Ski System
24 Glacier Creek Ski Tour
26 Bird Ridge
27 Indian Valley
27 Ship Creek to Indian
29 Old Johnson Trail
31 Flattop
32 The Ramp, to pass
34 Wolverine Peak
34 Wolverine Road
36 Rendezvous Peak
37 Eagle Lake
38 Dew Mound
39 Round Top and Black Tail Rocks
44 Reed Lakes
45 Hatcher Pass Ski Tour
48 Hicks Creek-Chitna Pass
49 Squaw Creek to Belanger Pass
50 Gunsight Mountain
51 Slide Mountain

LENGTH OF TRIP

Driving time is not considered in listing trip length.

SHORT (half-day or less)
1 Homer Beach Walk
3 Seven Lakes Trail, part of
4 Hidden Creek Trail
5 Skilak Lake Lookout Trail
6 Lower Fuller Lake
8 Lower Russian Lake
9 Carter Lake
9 Crescent Creek
10 Race Point
12 Ptarmigan Lake, west end
14 Juneau Falls
15 Palmer Creek
16 Hope Point Trail, first mile
18 Turnagain Pass Ski Tour
19 Byron Glacier View
20 Portage Lake Ski Tour
21 Portage Pass
22 Alyeska Glacier View
22 Alyeska Glacier View, from bottom
23 Alyeska Ski System
24 Glacier Creek Ski Tour
25 Girdwood Mine
26 Bird Ridge
28 Table Rock
29 Old Johnson Trail
31 Flattop
34 Wolverine Peak, to brushline
34 Wolverine Road in winter
36 Rendezvous Peak
38 Dew Mound
39 Black Tail Rocks
40 Thunderbird Falls
42 Bold Peak Valley
46 Craigie Creek
47 Peters Hills
51 Slide Mountain
53 McCarthy—Kennicott
54 Worthington Glacier Overlook
55 Mineral Creek

DAY TRIPS
1 Homer Beach Walk
3 Seven Lakes Trail
4, 7 Kenai River Trail-Hidden Creek Trail
4, 5 Skilak Lake Lookout Trail-Hidden Creek Trail
4, 5, 7 Kenai River Trail-Skilak Lake Lookout Trail
6 Fuller Lakes
7 Kenai River Canoe Trip, sections of
8 Lower Russian Lake and Cascades

9 Crescent Lake via Crescent Creek
9 Crescent Lake via Carter Lake
11 Lost Lake
11 Lost Lake to Primrose Creek
12 Ptarmigan Lake, west end
14 Caribou Creek cabin
14 Trout Lake cabin
15 Palmer Creek and beyond
16 Hope Point
17 Gull Rock
18 Turnagain Pass Ski Tour
21 Portage Pass
22 Mt. Alyeska, summit
22 Alyeska Glacier View from bottom
23 Winner Creek Gorge
24 Glacier Creek Ski Tour
25 Crow Pass
26 Bird Ridge
27 Indian Valley
28 Table Rock and beyond
29 Old Johnson Trail
30 Rabbit Lake
30 McHugh Peak via Rabbit Lake
31 Flattop and beyond
32 Powerline Pass
32 The Ramp
32 The Wedge
32, 27 The Ramp to Indian
33 Williwaw Lakes
34 Wolverine Peak
35 Knoya Peak
35 North Fork Campbell Creek
36 Rendezvous Peak and beyond
37 Eagle Lake
37 Eagle River Overlook
39 Black Tail Rocks
39 Round Top
39 Vista Peak
41 East Twin Pass
43 Lazy Mountain
44 Reed Lakes
45 Hatcher Pass Ski Tour
46 Craigie Creek and beyond
47 Peters Hills
48 Hicks Creek-Pinochle Creek Trail
48 Purinton Creek Trail
49 Belanger Pass
50 Gunsight Mountain in winter
51 Slide Mountain

STRENUOUS DAY TRIPS
6 Fuller Lakes ridge route
8 Cooper Lake-Russian Lakes
8 Upper Russian Lake
12 Ptarmigan Lake, east end
13 Johnson Pass

14 Devil's Pass Camp, via Summit Creek and Devil's Creek Trails
14 Juneau Lake
14 Swan Lake
16 Hope Point and beyond
23 Winner Creek Trail
26 Bird Ridge
28 McHugh Peak via Table Rock
35 Tikishla Peak
37 Eagle Lake and beyond
42 Bold Peak Valley
43 Matanuska Peak
47 Peters Hills

DAY TRIPS THAT MAKE OVERNIGHTS

3 Seven Lakes Trail
4 Hidden Creek Trail
4, 5, 7 Kenai River Trail-Skilak Lake Lookout Trail
6 Fuller Lakes
8 Lower Russian Lake
9 Crescent Lake (cabin)
11 Lost Lake
11 Lost Lake to Primrose Creek
12 Ptarmigan Lake, either end
14 Caribou Creek (cabin)
14 Trout Lake (cabin)
15 Palmer Creek
18 Turnagain Pass
21 Portage Pass
24 Glacier Creek Ski Tour
25 Crow Pass (cabin)
27 Indian Valley
30 Rabbit Lake
32 The Ramp
32, 27 The Ramp to Indian
33 Williwaw Lakes
35 Knoya Peak
35 North Fork Campbell Creek
37 Eagle Lake
41 East Twin Pass
42 Bold Peak Valley
44 Reed Lakes
46 Craigie Creek area
47 Peters Hills
49 Belanger Pass
50 Gunsight Mountain in winter
53 McCarthy—Kennicott

OVERNIGHT TRIPS

2 Swan Lake and Swanson River Canoe Routes
6 Fuller Lakes ridge route
7 Kenai River, sections of
8 Cooper Lake-Russian Lakes (cabin)
8 Upper Russian Lake (cabin)

13 Johnson Pass
14 Devil's Creek to Cooper Landing (cabin)
14 Devil's Pass Camp, via Summit Creek and Devil's Creek Trails (cabin)
14 East Creek (cabin)
14 Juneau Lake (cabin)
14 Swan Lake (cabin)
23 Winner Creek Trail
27 Ship Creek to Indian
30 Suicides
33, 35 North Fork Campbell Creek to Williwaw Lakes
35 Tikishla Peak
46 Craigie Creek and beyond
47 Peters Hills
48 Hicks Creek-Pinochle Creek Trail
48 Purinton Creek Trail
52 Gulkana River, lower section

TRIPS OF THREE DAYS OR MORE

2 Swan Lake and Swanson River Canoe Routes
7 Kenai River Canoe Trip
14 Resurrection Pass Trail System
25 Crow Pass to Eagle River
46 Craigie Creek and beyond
48 Hicks Creek-Chitna Pass
49 Squaw Creek to Belanger Pass
52 Gulkana River
53 Nikolai Ridge

CANOE OR KAYAK TRIPS

2 Swan Lake and Swanson River Canoe Routes
7 Kenai River Canoe Trip
52 Gulkana River

GOOD TRIPS FOR CHILDREN

1 Homer Beach Walk
2 Swan Lake and Swanson River Canoe Routes
3 Seven Lakes Trail
4 Hidden Creek Trail
5 Skilak Lake Lookout Trail
6 Fuller Lakes
8 Lower Russian Lake
9 Crescent Lake (overnight, cabin)
9 Crescent Lake via Carter Lake
11 Lost Lake (overnight)
12 Ptarmigan Lake, west end (overnight)

14 Juneau Falls
14 Resurrection Pass Trail System (5-day trip, cabins)
14 Caribou Creek (overnight, cabin)
14 Trout Lake (overnight, cabin)
15 Palmer Creek
16 Hope Point, first mile*
17 Gull Rock
18 Turnagain Pass in summer
18 Turnagain Pass Ski Tour
19 Byron Glacier View
20 Portage Lake Ski Tour
21 Portage Pass
22 Alyeska Glacier View
23 Alyeska Ski System
23 Winner Creek Gorge*
24 Glacier Creek Ski Tour
25 Crow Pass (overnight, cabin)
26 Bird Ridge*
27 Indian Valley
28 Table Rock

29 Old Johnson Trail
30 Rabbit Lake
31 Flattop*
32 The Ramp, to pass
32 The Wedge
36 Rendezvous Peak
38 Dew Mound
39 Round Top*
40 Thunderbird Falls
41 East Twin Pass (road)*
42 Bold Peak Valley*
43 Lazy Mountain*
46 Craigie Creek
47 Peters Hills
51 Slide Mountain, west trail, 2 miles
53 McCarthy—Kennicott
54 Worthington Glacier Overlook, first half-mile

*These trips are more difficult (usually steeper), but are recommended for experienced children.

TRIPS ACCESSIBLE BY PUBLIC TRANSPORTATION

The following trips may be reached by bus, train, or ferry, though daily service or year-round service may not be available. If side-road distances are short, worthwhile trips off the main bus lines are included. Additional miles one way are noted. Transportation services are:

(1) Transportation Services, Inc., 1040 E. 1st, Anchorage, Ak., 99501, 272-5592; serves Kenai Peninsula, including Seward, Soldotna, Kenai, and Homer; Mt. Alyeska in winter; Fairbanks and Valdez.

(2) Alaska-Yukon Motorcoaches, 327 F St., Anchorage, Ak., 99501, 276-2155; serves Tok, Valdez.

(3) Alaska Railroad, Traffic Division, Pouch 7-2111, Anchorage, Ak., 99510, 265-2494; serves Fairbanks, Seward, and Whittier. May be flag stop, requiring advance notice.

(4) Alaska State Ferry System, Box 2344, Anchorage, Ak., 99510, 272-4482; serves Valdez, Whittier.

(5) People Mover, 3500 Tudor Road, Anchorage, Ak., 99502, 272-4411.

1 Homer Beach Walk (1)
3 Seven Lakes Trail (1)
4, 7 Kenai River Trail (1) + 1 mile
6 Fuller Lakes (1)
7 Kenai River (raft or folding boat) (1)
8 Russian Lakes (1)
9 Crescent Lake (1) +3½ miles
9 Carter Lake (1)
10 Race Point (1)
11 Lost Lake (1)
12 Ptarmigan Lake (1)
13 Johnson Pass (1)
14 Resurrection Pass Trail System (1)
18 Turnagain Pass (1)
21 Portage Pass (3) (4)
22 Alyeska Glacier View (1) (3) + 3 miles
23 Winner Creek Gorge (1) (3) + 3 miles; (1) in winter
24 Glacier Creek Ski Tour (1)
25 Crow Pass (1) (3) + 7½ miles
26 Bird Ridge (1) (3)
27 Indian Valley (1) (3) + 1 mile

28 Table Rock (1) (3)
29 Old Johnson Trail (1) (3)
30 Rabbit Lake (5) + 6 miles
31 Flattop (5) + 4.5 miles
32 Ramp (5) + 4.5 miles
33 Williwaw Lakes (5) + 4.5 miles
34 Wolverine Peak (5) + 2.6 miles
35 Knoya-Tikishla (5) + 2.6 miles
36 Rendezvous Peak (5) + 7 miles
37 Eagle Lake (5) + 7 miles
49 Round Top (1) (2) + 4 miles
40 Thunderbird Falls (1) (2)
43 Lazy Mountain (1) (2) + 3½ miles
48 Hicks Creek-Chitna Pass (1) (2)
49 Squaw Creek to Belanger Pass (1) (2)
50 Gunsight Mountain (1) (2)
51 Slide Mountain (1) (2)
52 Gulkana River (by raft or folding boat) (1) (2)
54 Worthington Glacier Overlook (1) (2)
55 Mineral Creek (4) + 5½ miles

Organizations Concerned about Alaska's Future

Activist organizations:

Upper Cook Inlet Chapter, ACS
Box 3395
Anchorage, Alaska 99510

Alaska Conservation Society (ACS)
Box 80192
College, Alaska 99701
(parent society which can put you in touch
with other chapters)

Friends of the Earth
Box 1796
Fairbanks, Alaska 99707

Sierra Club, Alaska Chapter
Box 2025
Anchorage, Alaska 99510

Educational, tax deductible organizations:

Alaska Center for the Environment
913 W. 6th Ave.
Anchorage, Alaska 99501

Fairbanks Environmental Center
Box 1796
Fairbanks, Alaska 99707

**Special interest organizations with a
conservation concern:**

Mountaineering Club of Alaska
Box 2037
Anchorage, Alaska 99510

Anchorage Audubon Society
Box 1161
Anchorage, Alaska 99510

National organizations:

Sierra Club
530 Bush Street
San Francisco, California 94108

Friends of the Earth
529 Commercial
San Francisco, California 94111

Wilderness Society
1901 Pennsylvania Ave., NW
Washington, D.C. 20006

National Audubon Society
950 Third Avenue
New York, New York 10022

INDEX